Independence & Empire

Independence & Empire

The New South's Cotton Mill Campaign

1865–1901

Patrick J. Hearden

DeKalb
Northern Illinois University Press

Chapter 6; "New England's Reaction to the New South," is reprinted in revised form with permission of the *South Atlantic Quarterly*. Copyright 1976, Duke University Press (Durham, North Carolina).

Library of Congress Cataloging in Publication Data

Hearden, Patrick J., 1942-
  Independence & empire.

  Bibliography: p.
  Includes index.
  1. Cotton trade—Southern States—History—
19th century. 2. Textile industry—Southern
States—History—19th century. 3. Southern States
—Economic conditions. 4. Reconstruction. I. Title.
II. Title: Independence and empire.
HD9877.A13H4   338.4'767721'0975   82-2283
ISBN 0-87580-083-1   AACR2
ISBN 0-87580-535-3 (pbk.)

For My Mother

The significance of the section in American history is that it is a faint image of a European nation and that we need to reexamine our history in light of this fact. Our politics and our society have been shaped by sectional complexity and interplay not unlike what goes on between European nations.

Frederick Jackson Turner, 1925

*C*ontents

Acknowledgments

The community of scholars at the University of Wisconsin provided a hothouse for my intellectual development. Robert H. Van Meter sparked my original interest in history and inspired me with his social commitment. William Appleman Williams directed my investigation of the New South's quest for economic independence and commercial empire as it evolved from a seminar paper into a doctoral dissertation. Professor Williams stimulated me with his ideas, supported me with his funds, and sustained me with his friendship. Allen G. Bogue, John M. Cooper, Avery O. Craven, Stanley I. Kutler, Thomas J. McCormick, Morton Rothstein, Richard H. Sewell, and Robert S. Starobin gave me the benefit of their criticism and their encouragement.

Charles B. Dew of Williams College, Harold M. Hyman of Rice University, and Carl P. Parrini of Northern Illinois University read my entire manuscript and offered valuable advice. William C. Lloyd and J. Michael Thorn suggested useful stylistic changes.

The library and manuscript staffs of the following institutions made my research more fruitful: Alabama State Department of Archives and History, Center for Research Libraries, Clemson University, Duke University, Harvard Graduate School of Business, Library of Congress, Massachusetts Historical Society, Mississippi State Department of Archives and History, National Archives of the United States, State Historical Society of Wisconsin, University of North Carolina, and the University of South Carolina.

A fellowship from the University of Wisconsin and a grant from the University of Missouri helped finance my study.

Madison, Wisconsin
January 1982

PJH

Preface

*T*his study began with a simple hypothesis: spokesmen for the cotton textile industry attempted to influence the conduct of American diplomacy during the last three decades of the nineteenth century. I assumed at the outset that New England would be the focal point of my investigation, but the primary documents soon turned my attention to the South.

I found that most northern cotton manufacturers, especially those producing finer cloth in lower New England, exhibited only sporadic interest in overseas economic expansion. Many who dumped their surplus goods abroad during periods of depression abandoned the foreign market when prosperity returned at home. Southern mill owners, on the other hand, manufactured coarse fabrics almost exclusively; and they maintained their export orientation regardless of fluctuations in the business cycle. Moreover, these southern textile executives and their political representatives did in fact exert pressure upon the federal government for the protection and extension of their foreign commerce.

The evidence both confirmed my original hypothesis and enlarged the scope of my project. It became clear that the drive to bring the cotton factories to the cotton fields was a vital part of a larger endeavor to promote sectional economic development in the decades following the Civil War. Southerners regarded cotton manufacturing as a pioneer industry that would blaze the trail for the introduction of related business concerns. They believed that the rise of urban communities would in turn create local markets for diversified agriculture and thereby enable their region to obtain relief from the burdens of a one crop economy.

This knowledge opened up a tempting avenue of research, but I rejected the option of embarking upon a sweeping examination

of all phases of the southern industrial crusade. I decided instead
to continue my concentration on cotton manufacturing in the hope
of providing a window through which the broader struggle for
sectional economic growth could be viewed. Hence I undertook
the task of writing a history of the New South movement as it
related to the cotton textile industry.

While not motivated by the spirit of revisionism, I gradually
discovered that the standard interpretations of the New South
demanded drastic alteration. The works of Broadus Mitchell and
Paul H. Buck maintain that nationalism and industrialism were
integrated in southern thinking, but primary data convinced me
that the reverse was really true. Over and over again southerners
advocated factory construction as a way of defeating the hated
Yankees, and they repeatedly charged that their northern rivals
were maneuvering to retard their industrial development. Despite
the tendency among historians to discount these accusations,
many New England leaders actually did try to undermine the New
South's fight for economic self-sufficiency. Thus, rather than a
movement toward sectional reunion, the southern cotton mill
campaign was a continuation of the battle that, in its military
phase, had been lost in 1865.

My research, furthermore, contradicts the arguments advanced
by William B. Hesseltine and C. Vann Woodward. These influential
scholars depict the South in terms of a fundamental antagonism
between town and country. Southern entrepreneurs and their
political allies are portrayed as colonial agents for northern
economic penetration, while southern agrarians are cast as
backward-looking provincials with an anti-industrial attitude that
culminated in Populism. The southern states did experience their
share of discord between urban and rural elements. But it is also
true that factory masters hoped to foster the wealth and welfare of
their region, while commercial farmers and planters participated
in the cotton mill crusade. Indeed, a solid pro-industrial consensus
united agricultural businessmen and their metropolitan colleagues and laid the foundations for the New South program.

Although my research centered on the last third of the nineteenth century, it became evident that the main themes of my
study extended far beyond that period. Secondary sources indicate
that almost everything that happened after the Civil War had been
rehearsed before that epic contest. I therefore propose in Chapter
1 that the antebellum era provided a prologue to the New South

movement. It is likewise the case that neither the sectional conflict nor the effort to shape foreign policy ended with the Spanish-American War. Thus I conclude with the suggestion that the twentieth century has served as an epilogue to the New South's quest for economic independence and commercial empire.

This study does not propose to test the rationality of the New South's attempt to establish a textile industry as a base for attaining general economic development. Yet it is evident that the leaders of the cotton mill campaign in the southern states responded in a reasonable way to their material environment. Given an apparent shortage of capital and an abundant supply of cheap labor, it was quite sensible for southerners to construct textile factories as the first step in their drive for broader industrial growth. Southern leaders did not see any alternatives open to them. Nor were they alone in this regard. Many contemporaries, including the Japanese, embarked upon similar programs for economic development. The southerners were not as successful as their Far Eastern counterparts in achieving their long-range objectives, but they did make impressive gains.

The arrangement of my material follows a topical rather than a strict chronological pattern. My decision to emphasize my main themes without confining myself to a straightforward narrative scheme has resulted in some unavoidable redundancy. Yet the advantages of the organization would seem to outweigh its defects. The repetitive nature of the presentation enables the reader to view the same issues or events from different perspectives. Hence the approach should strengthen the argument and sharpen the analysis.

Independence & Empire

A small quantity of manufactured produce purchases a great quantity of rude produce.

Adam Smith, Political Economist, 1776

The shuttle and the loom, operating on the products of your fields and your flocks, will in this century emancipate you from commercial thralldom, as the operations of your arsenals and foundries delivered you, in the last, from political slavery.

William Loughton Smith, Political Leader, 1808

Southern Domestic Manufactures—May the time soon arrive when South Carolina shall no longer be dependent on her Tariff Sisters for food or clothing.

Fourth of July Toast, 1828

Cotton manufactures have been the pioneers which have introduced and given impetus to all other branches of mechanism in Great Britain, the continent of Europe, and this country.

William Gregg, Factory Master, 1844

This branch of manufactures should be extended until the markets of the whole world are supplied with cotton yarn and coarse fabrics produced in the manufactories of the Southern States.

James L. Orr, Congressman, 1855

The South stands in the same relation to New England now, that we as a nation did to Old England fifty years ago, if it was good policy for us then, as a nation, to adopt and support a general system of manufacturing the same policy is equally good now when applied to the South.

J. M. Wesson, Textile Executive, 1858

Show Brother Jonathan that we have changed our tactics, and that, in the future, we are to meet him in battle array—in the great field of commerce and home industry, where we intend to fight to the death against every attempt at usurpation.

William Gregg, 1860

1

Antebellum Origins of the New South

The antebellum era serves as a prologue to the New South's epic quest for economic independence and commercial empire. In the years before the Civil War, a group of prominent southerners gave birth to an ideology that viewed progress as a product of industrial growth. They believed that the rise of cotton mills would attract related enterprises and that the subsequent urban expansion would encourage agricultural diversification by increasing the local demand for foodstuffs. Southern factory backers hoped to export finished goods rather than raw materials to cure the ills of a one crop economy and to achieve prosperity and power. Their program for a new order, which would emerge in full dress in the postwar decades, began to take shape during the first half of the nineteenth century.

Southern ambitions for industrial development had their roots in early American struggles to shake loose from material subservience to Great Britain. Although English rulers acknowledged the political independence of their former colonies, they were still intent on retaining the United States as an economic vassal. The intellectual framework for their policy had been formulated in 1776 by Adam Smith in his treatise, *The Wealth of Nations*. Smith argued that metropolitan areas have a natural advantage in trading with agrarian regions because "a small quantity of manufactured produce purchases a great quantity of rude produce."[1] Acting on that analysis, the British tried to prevent the new Amer-

---

[1] Adam Smith, *The Wealth of Nations* (New York: Random House, Modern Library, 1937), p. 642.

ican nation from acquiring machinery needed for the development of its nascent textile industry. They aimed to keep the United States on the agricultural half of an imperial relationship with industrial England.

Americans resented the idea that, despite their political emancipation, they should remain colonials in an economic sense. They aspired to organize an integrated system of agriculture, commerce, and manufacturing in order to become self-sufficient and thereby complete their revolution against the mother country. British interference with their lucrative overseas trade after 1805 reinforced their desire for a balanced economy. Northern merchants who had accumulated capital by engaging in foreign commerce sought a domestic outlet for their surplus funds, and the growing hostility toward England made investment in home industry a patriotic venture. These considerations prompted Americans to launch an energetic cotton mill campaign in an effort to attain economic independence.

Southerners eagerly participated in this endeavor to break the chains of a colonial economy. Those who raised staple crops for export believed that the British maritime restrictions were causing a decline in cotton and tobacco prices. The agricultural depression between 1808 and 1812 and the concomitant animosity toward England aroused great interest in industrial expansion. Newspapers from Maryland to Georgia encouraged investment in domestic manufacturing with appeals that tied individual profit to national patriotism. Eminent planters and affluent businessmen organized textile firms, and state legislatures exhibited their approval by granting charters for the new undertakings. As the mill fever spread from the tidewater into the backcountry, cotton factories were erected in every southern state.[2]

The establishment of the Columbia Manufacturing Company dramatizes the close connection between the southern mill boom and the battle to escape from the confines of economic bondage.

---

[2] Richard W. Griffin, "Origins of Southern Cotton Manufactures, 1807–1816," *Cotton History Review* 1 (January 1960): 6–7; Richard W. Griffin, "Ante Bellum Industrial Foundations of the (Alleged) 'New South,' " *Textile History Review* 5 (April 1964): 37; Ernest M. Lander, Jr., *The Textile Industry in Antebellum South Carolina* (Baton Rouge: Louisiana State University Press, 1969), pp. 4–12; and Marjorie S. Mendenhall, "A History of Agriculture in South Carolina, 1790–1860: An Economic and Social Study" (Ph.D. dissertation, University of North Carolina, 1940), pp. 20–25.

Washington businessmen announced plans in 1808 to build a cotton factory in the nation's capital, and they made their purposes explicit at the organizational meeting. The British Empire, these industrial promoters complained, had imposed a mighty system of commercial repression designed to "reduce us to a state of colonial subjection." The Washingtonians proclaimed that it was "the dictate of the soundest patriotism to render ourselves independent of the workshops of Europe." Hence they reasoned that every section of the country had a duty to foster "the establishment and extension of domestic manufactures."[3]

The organization of the South Carolina Homespun Company similarly illustrates the intimate linkage between southern industrial activity and the crusade for economic liberation. The stockholders successfully petitioned the South Carolina General Assembly in 1808 for an act of incorporation permitting them to erect a textile enterprise in Charleston. Their request emphasized their intention to place the country beyond "the paralyzing touch or control of any Foreign power." Former Congressman William Loughton Smith reiterated this aim in his keynote address given at the laying of the cornerstone of the new Charleston concern. "The shuttle and the loom," he declared, "will in this century emancipate you from commercial thralldom, as the operations of your arsenals and foundries delivered you, in the last, from political slavery."[4]

English manufacturers watched the rise of spinning and weaving establishments in the United States with worried eyes. They had no wish to suffer a permanent loss of the American market for their own yarn and cloth. Thus, as soon as the War of 1812 ended and normal commercial intercourse resumed, the British started flooding the United States with cheap fabrics in an attempt to stifle the burgeoning textile business. American manufacturing interests immediately demanded relief from this destructive competition. Representative John C. Calhoun of South Carolina

---

[3] Richard W. Griffin, "The Columbia Manufacturing Company and the Textile Industry of the District of Columbia, 1808–1816," *Maryland Historical Magazine* 57 (September 1962): 261.

[4] For the full text of the speech by Smith, see *Cotton History Review* 1 (July 1960): 138–42. See also Lander, *The Textile Industry in Antebellum South Carolina*, p. 8; and George C. Rogers, Jr., *Evolution of a Federalist: William Loughton Smith of Charleston, 1758–1812* (Columbia: University of South Carolina Press, 1962), pp. 376–77, 393.

responded in 1816 by introducing a tariff bill in Congress, and southerners joined with northerners in helping to pass the measure calculated to protect the country's infant industries.

Between 1815 and 1819, however, two basic phenomena produced a crucial shift in southern orientation. First, the British dumping policy did severe damage to the American textile industry. The larger New England firms, blessed with solid financial backing, survived the onslaught and even expanded operations under the cover of the tariff. But the smaller mills in the South were hit hard, and many shut down. Second, the steadily increasing price of cotton made manufacturing seem less attractive than planting. These circumstances led more and more southerners to commit themselves to the cultivation of a few primary crops and to abandon their interest in an integrated economy.

Nor in the beginning did this move away from manufacturing appear unwise, as the South basked in prosperity during the years immediately following the war. But this happy condition ended abruptly with the panic of 1819 and the ensuing agricultural depression. The main cause of the hard times lay in the expansion of cotton culture into the newer and more fertile territory in the Southwest. The subsequent jump in production resulted in a drop in cotton prices which in turn stimulated a population movement away from the worn lands in the Southeast. A similar decline in tobacco prices added to the economic troubles that plagued the South Atlantic states for more than a decade.[5]

The South became increasingly alienated from the North during the agricultural depression in the 1820s. Northern maneuvers to raise the tariff on industrial articles, coupled with the budding anti-slavery movement, provoked strong feelings of resentment in the southern states. Though political leaders like Calhoun had helped establish the principle of protection, it was not long before most southerners concluded that elevated import duties presented a dual threat to their section. High tariff rates would force farmers and planters to pay more money for many items that they needed but did not produce for themselves. They would also irritate foreigners and thereby make it harder to penetrate overseas markets for staple crops.[6]

---

[5] Alfred G. Smith, Jr., *Economic Readjustment of an Old Cotton State: South Carolina, 1820–1860* (Columbia: University of South Carolina Press, 1958), pp. 4–7, 25–38.

[6] Charles S. Sydnor, *The Development of Southern Sectionalism, 1819–1848* (Baton Rouge: Louisiana State University Press, 1948), pp. 134–56; William W.

Despite their renunciation of the high tariff policy, southerners began a long struggle in the late 1820s to balance their own economy. Even the many South Carolinians who wanted to nullify the tariff became inflamed with cotton mill fever.[7] Southerners believed that textile establishments would produce handsome dividends for stockholders and that the factory hands would provide a local market for grain and meat. Distress in the countryside sparked the initial interest in cotton manufacturing and diversified farming, and the growing enmity toward the North sharpened the desire to achieve sectional economic independence. In short, southerners aspired to become self-sufficient in order to regain their lost prosperity and to retaliate against their Yankee adversaries.

The consequent cotton mill campaign that swept across the South Atlantic states displayed similar characteristics to the earlier industrial crusade except for one striking difference: sectional patriotism had replaced love of country. Now southerners were directing their bitterness toward New England rather than Great Britain. A North Carolina newspaper, for instance, advocated the construction of textile enterprises in 1828 as a way to "buffet the northern manufacturers with their own weapons."[8] In the same year, the Richland Volunteer Rifle Club voiced the sentiments of a great many in the Palmeto State when it celebrated the Fourth of July with the following toast: "Southern Domestic Manufactures— May the time soon arrive when South Carolina shall no longer be dependent on her Tariff Sisters for food or clothing."[9] As the agita-

---

Freehling, *Prelude to Civil War: The Nullification Controversy in South Carolina, 1816–1836* (New York: Harper & Row, 1965), pp. 89–133.

[7] The nullification debate marked a significant shift in economic attitudes in South Carolina. Many urged a more diversified state economy, and it became patriotic for gentlemen to take part in manufacturing and commerce. Wealthy planters invested in East Bay countinghouses, and by the end of the 1830s permanent residents had assumed control of Charleston's mercantile affairs. Leading nullifiers like George McDuffie, Dr. Thomas Cooper, and Franklin H. Elmore purchased stock in new manufacturing establishments. Outspoken unionists such as David R. Williams likewise invested funds in industrial enterprises. (See Ernest M. Lander, Jr., "The Iron Industry in Ante-Bellum South Carolina," *Journal of Southern History* 20 [August 1954]: 342–43; Harvey T. Cook, *The Life and Legacy of David Rogerson Williams* [New York, 1916], pp. 271, 331; Freehling, *Prelude to Civil War,* pp. 304–5; and Lander, *The Textile Industry in Antebellum South Carolina,* pp. 32–38.)

[8] *Tarborough Free Press,* as quoted in *Niles' Register,* May 10, 1828, p. 175.

[9] Smith, *Economic Readjustment of an Old Cotton State,* p. 113.

tion mounted between 1828 and 1832, the Southeast experienced a cotton mill boom.[10]

Southern industrial activity, however, continued to fluctuate with changing circumstances. In the 1830s, an increase in cotton prices, combined with a decline in sectional antagonism following a tariff compromise, retarded investment in textile manufacturing. But the situation was soon reversed. A downward spiral in the price of cotton commenced as the decade came to a close, and the ills that afflicted southern agriculture persisted for more than ten years. The rising tide of abolitionism and the great debate over the expansion of slavery into the territories added to the anxiety in Dixie. The consequent desire to strike back at the North and to restore prosperity to the South triggered still another cotton mill boom between 1845 and 1850.

The revival of southern interest in home industry during the agricultural depression in the 1840s was extensive. Some still blamed the tariff for their difficulties, but the long period of low prices led the majority to conclude that the fundamental cause of their problems lay in the overproduction of cotton. As economic diversification became the most commonly proposed solution, a third round of cotton mill fever broke out in the Southeast.[11] It generated more excitement than the previous epidemics and spread into the Southwest after the drop in staple prices brought hard times to that region. As a result, newspapers from Virginia to Arkansas sponsored the drive to cast off the shackles of a colonial economy.[12]

A long series of southern commercial conventions, stemming from the depression, reflected this renewed concern for cotton

---

[10] Richard W. Griffin, "The Fisher Committee Report to the North Carolina General Assembly, 1828," *Cotton History Review* 2 (January 1961): 52–67; Griffin, "Ante Bellum Industrial Foundations of the (Alleged) 'New South,'" pp. 39–40; and Norris W. Preyer, "The Historian, the Slave, and the Ante-Bellum Textile Industry," *Journal of Negro History* 46 (April 1961): 72–73.

[11] Robert R. Russell, *Economic Aspects of Southern Sectionalism, 1840–1861* (Urbana: University of Illinois Press, 1924), pp. 289–90; John G. Van Deusen, *Economic Basis of Disunion in South Carolina* (New York: Columbia University Studies in History, 1928), pp. 262–64; and Ernest F. Patterson, "Cotton, the First Problem of United States Agriculture," *Cotton History Review* 1 (October 1960): 159–61.

[12] Sydnor, *Development of Southern Sectionalism*, pp. 255–66; Richard W. Griffin, "Pro-Industrial Sentiment and Cotton Factories in Arkansas, 1820–1863," *Arkansas Historical Quarterly* 15 (Summer 1956): 127.

manufacturing and mixed farming. The first group of meetings stressed the value of establishing direct trade between the South and Europe. They issued bitter complaints that the New York merchants were siphoning off an unfair share of the profits derived from the exportation of their leading staples. While their commitment to achieving southern commercial independence remained strong, these conventions increasingly urged agricultural diversification and industrial expansion. Some explicitly tied these proposals together by arguing that direct trade would help their section amass funds for investment in farms and factories.[13]

Wealthy planters played an active role in the movement to establish an integrated economy in the South. Rural nabobs often joined urban businessmen in supplying money for the erection of cotton factories.[14] Agricultural participation in the industrial crusade became institutionalized when the harsh depression stirred planters to begin holding their own meetings. Concerned originally with obtaining higher prices for cotton, these planters' conventions soon turned their attention to the same subjects that had captivated the commercial conventions.[15] Agrarian organizations operating on a smaller scale likewise backed the push for a balanced economy. During the 1840s, for example, more than half of the speeches delivered before the State Agricultural Society of South Carolina advocated home industry. In customary manner, the association resolved in 1844 that "a combined system of Agriculture, Manufactures, and Commerce is essential in promoting the prosperity and happiness of a community."[16]

It was during this depression decade that the ideology which would later direct the New South's thrust for economic independence and commercial empire began to assume form. A prominent group of antebellum leaders were inspired by a grand vision of history that explained the ascent of strong nation states in terms

---

[13] Herbert Wender, *Southern Commercial Conventions, 1837–1859* (Baltimore: Johns Hopkins Press, 1930); and Russell, *Economic Aspects of Southern Sectionalism*, p. 99.

[14] Eugene D. Genovese, *The Political Economy of Slavery* (New York: Random House, 1965); p. 188; Robert S. Starobin, *Industrial Slavery in the Old South* (New York: Oxford University Press, 1970), pp. 206–14; and John H. Napier III, "Judge Edward McGehee: Cotton Planter, Pioneer Manufacturer and Mississippi Philanthropist," *Cotton History Review* 1 (January 1960): 27–28.

[15] Weymouth T. Jordan, *Rebels in the Making: Planters' Conventions and Southern Propaganda* (Tuscaloosa, Ala.: Confederate Publishing, 1958).

[16] Lander, *The Textile Industry in Antebellum South Carolina*, p. 51.

of industrial growth. Governor James H. Hammond of South Carolina declared in 1849 that past experience demonstrated that "those nations only are powerful and wealthy, which in addition to agriculture, devote themselves to commerce and manufactures." Like many other patrons of industry, Hammond wished that southerners would be "guided by the light of history" and diversify their economic pursuits so that their region could participate in the scramble for wealth and power.[17]

The spokesmen for a new order always regarded cotton mills as the initiators of material advancement. William Gregg, soon to become an outstanding factory master in the Old South, proclaimed in 1844 that "cotton manufactures have been the pioneers which have introduced and given impetus to all other branches of mechanism in Great Britain, the continent of Europe, and this country."[18] James H. Taylor, another notable industrialist, drew the same lesson from history. Besides providing a local market for provisions, he asserted in 1849, spinning and weaving establishments would "give employment to almost every kind of industry."[19] Others like Governor Hammond agreed that the conversion of cotton into cloth would "lay the foundation" for general economic improvement. Accordingly, he advised southerners to take advantage of their natural resources and to follow the example of both Old England and New England.[20]

These forerunners of the New South viewed foreign trade as a central element in their program for economic development. They did not recommend a radical change away from plantation slavery to reduce rural poverty and to increase the local demand for manufactured articles.[21] They looked instead to foreign sales to stimulate cotton mill building and thereby to create a home market for

---

[17] *De Bow's Review*, June 1850, pp. 503–5; see also January 1850, pp. 1–20.

[18] William Gregg, *Essays on Domestic Industry*. First published as a series of twelve articles in the *Charleston Courier* between September 20 and December 11, 1844, these articles have been conveniently reprinted as an appendix to Daniel A. Tompkins, *Cotton Mill, Commercial Features* (Charlotte: Presses Observer Printing House, 1899), pp. 207–35.

[19] *De Bow's Review*, January 1850, p. 27.

[20] *De Bow's Review*, June 1850, p. 508. For an excellent discussion of the leading role textiles played in the economic development of the Northeast see Douglass C. North, *The Economic Growth of the United States, 1790–1860* (New York: W. W. Norton, 1966), pp. 159–62.

[21] Genovese, *The Political Economy of Slavery*, pp. 180–208.

farm produce. Southerners were confident that their abundant supplies of crude material, water power, and cheap labor would enable them to compete successfully for the cotton goods trade of the world. They aimed to export rough fabrics rather than raw fibers in order to overcome their colonial status and to march along the road to commercial empire.

Southern industrial promoters repeatedly linked the rise of cotton mills in their section to overseas economic expansion. James H. Hammond maintained in 1849 that "a foreign market would be indispensable" for southern cotton manufacturing to realize its full potential.[22] In the same year, a Georgia newspaper predicted that the state would become a great textile center because it had the ability to produce cloth at a very low cost. "This must necessarily give us the advantage in the markets of the world," it boasted, "and this advantage will soon cause factories to spring up in almost every county."[23] Georgia was already shipping cotton goods to China; and, hoping to enlarge this business, the paper called for the construction of a southern transcontinental railroad.[24] J. D. B. De Bow, the influential New Orleans journalist and industrial booster, concurred that a southern route to the Pacific was needed for "commercial Empire."[25]

But, more than any other statement, William Gregg's highly praised and widely circulated *Essays on Domestic Industry,* published in 1844, provides a classic document of the emerging New South world view. Gregg persuasively argued that his section's colonial condition was due to the lack of factories and not to the existence of the tariff. In the process, he quoted a southern periodical to underscore his belief in Adam Smith's pronouncement that specie generally flows from agricultural areas toward industrial communities: "No nation ever became wealthy by raising the raw material and then exchanging it for the manufactured article. The manufacturing people always have the advantage." He reasoned that textile enterprises would attract other industries, as well as create a local market for foodstuffs, and consequently change the South's unfavorable trade relationship with the North.

---

[22] *De Bow's Review,* June 1850, p. 509.

[23] *De Bow's Review,* January 1850, pp. 39–43.

[24] Richard W. Griffin, "The Origins of the Industrial Revolution in Georgia: Cotton Textiles, 1810–1865," *Georgia Historical Quarterly* 42 (December 1958): 365.

[25] *De Bow's Review,* July 1849, pp. 1–38.

Gregg then outlined the basic strategy for the cotton mill campaign. Southerners should at first concentrate on taking the coarse cloth business away from northerners. After achieving that victory, the South could begin to challenge New England in the manufacture of finer fabrics. Southerners, moreover, should produce export goods like heavy sheetings, shirtings, and drills. "As the home market is already over-supplied," Gregg emphasized, "the capitalists now embarking in the business cannot look to anything but foreign trade for the consumption of their fabrics." If every cotton factory in South Carolina shipped its entire output abroad, he assured, "it would scarcely be felt in the market of the world."[26] A bit later, Gregg put his precepts into practice when he built the famous Graniteville Manufacturing Company as a model mill, and before long his firm commenced exporting sheetings to the China market.

Nevertheless, despite the widespread enthusiasm for economic diversification, some southerners did criticize the cotton mill campaign. The traditional association between manufacturing and protection aroused fears that industrial growth would generate a powerful tariff lobby in the South. The supporters of factory construction tried to put these apprehensions to rest. They pointed out that high import duties would not be necessary for the coarse cloth that they planned to produce in their section. They further explained that their ambitions extended far beyond the narrow domestic field, since their mill building program depended upon foreign commerce. In short, they insisted that expansion abroad rather than protection at home provided the key to southern economic development.[27]

Some southerners, however, worried that industrialization would create a proletarian class hostile to the slave system. Though most believed that manufacturing was desirable, a debate arose over the relative dangers of white and black labor. One group, headed by Gregg, Taylor, and Hammond, advocated the employment of white mill hands and cautioned that slaves would be difficult to control in factories. Christopher G. Memminger led

---

[26] Gregg, *Essays on Domestic Industry*, in Tompkins, *Cotton Mill*, pp. 230, 210, 232.

[27] Chauncey S. Boucher, *The Antebellum Attitudes of South Carolina toward Manufacturing and Agriculture* (St. Louis: Washington University Studies, 1916), pp. 250–54; and Philip G. Davidson, "Industrialism in the Ante-Bellum South," *South Atlantic Quarterly* 27 (October 1928): 412–13.

an opposing group that favored industrial slavery and fretted that white workers might become abolitionists. Some hoped that the exploitation of slaves in factories would help offset the North's capital advantage and thereby enable their section to compete successfully in manufacturing. The practical compromise foreshadowed the arrangement that would prevail later during the New South era. Most antebellum industries used slaves, but the upcountry cotton mills generally employed white operatives.[28]

Despite these differences in opinion regarding industrial workers, nearly everyone agreed that slavery should remain a central feature in southern life. Even those who preferred white labor expressed growing concern that the federal government would interfere with their peculiar institution. "We are under the impression here," William Gregg wrote a Boston manufacturer in 1850, "that the spirit of abolition is becoming so high with you that it will override the politicians and wise men of the country." He warned that southerners would not tolerate any outside meddling in their domestic affairs. "With us," he explained, "slaves are property, and it amounts to many millions, the protection and free use of which is guaranteed to us by the Constitution, without that protection the Union is of no use to us."[29]

Southern mill building suffered more from a rise in cotton prices in the early 1850s than from apprehensions about any possible baneful effects of industrialization. On the one hand, the increased cost of the raw material made it more difficult for small southern factories to compete with bigger northern firms possessing abundant financial reserves. Many textile companies in the South failed, and reports of large dividends disappeared from the newspapers. On the other hand, the upturn in the demand for the fleecy white staple brought renewed prosperity to planters and reduced their inclination to break old investment habits and risk their money in uncertain business ventures. As cotton prices held rather high for the rest of the decade, agriculture continued to outbid manufacturing for capital, and southern industrial growth remained limited.[30]

The evidence contradicts the argument advanced by Eugene D.

---

[28] Starobin, *Industrial Slavery in the Old South*, pp. 206–14.

[29] William Gregg to Amos A. Lawrence, September 2, 1850, Lawrence Correspondence, Massachusetts Historical Society, Boston.

[30] Russell, *Economic Aspects of Southern Sectionalism*, pp. 58–59; and Van Deusen, *Economic Basis of Disunion in South Carolina*, p. 285.

Genovese in *The Political Economy of Slavery* that the precapitalist mentality of the planter class prevented the Old South from establishing a general system of manufacturing. Actually it was precisely their capitalist nature which discouraged the lords of the lash from putting more of their money in industry. Recent historical scholarship indicates that cotton culture yielded as high a return as any alternative investment available in Dixie.[31] Southern planters were agricultural businessmen who responded to marketplace incentives much like their metropolitan neighbors in the North. While declining profits in commerce spurred many northern merchants to become manufacturers, pecuniary considerations induced most southern planters to remain agrarian entrepreneurs. They continued to invest in land and slaves despite the widespread belief that industrial development would benefit their region as a whole. In other words, their desire for personal wealth outweighed their commitment to sectional welfare.

But the intensification of the sectional conflict during the 1850s, centering on the issue of expanding slavery, did produce increasing agitation in behalf of economic diversification in the South. *De Bow's Review,* for example, ardently commended plans for the establishment of a textile factory in Louisiana in 1857 as "the proper way to fight the North, and the course to pursue if we would secure our Southern independence."[32] Congressman James L. Orr of South Carolina made the same argument and tied his plea for more cotton mills to overseas commercial expansion. "This branch of manufactures should be extended," he exhorted, "until the markets of the whole world are supplied with cotton yarn and coarse fabrics produced in the manufactories of the Southern States."[33]

Prominent cotton mill managers spearheaded the drive for southern economic independence. Enoch Steadman, the superintendent of a Tennessee factory, urged the establishment of "a general system of manufacturing" in 1858 because he believed that the laws of political economy dictated that southerners must

---

[31] See, for example, *Agricultural History* 44 (January 1970) and 49 (April 1975).

[32] *De Bow's Review,* January 1857, p. 110. For similar expressions of the mounting agitation for southern economic independence, see Weymouth T. Jordan, *Ante Bellum Alabama: Town and Country* (Tallahassee: Florida State University, 1957), pp. 140–60.

[33] *Charleston Daily Courier,* April 18, 1855.

process their own staples to become prosperous and powerful.[34] Many other textile executives, like President J. M. Wesson of the Mississippi Manufacturing Company, agreed that southerners needed to industrialize in order to transcend their colonial status. "The South stands in the same relation to New England now, that we as a nation did to Old England fifty years ago," Wesson wrote; "if it was good policy for us then, as a nation, to adopt and support a general system of manufacturing the same policy is equally good now when applied to the South."[35]

Proponents of a new order also began thinking that secession would help them realize their long cherished dream of economic self-sufficiency. They hoped that disunion would prod their section to rely less upon foodstuffs from the Northwest and manufactures from the Northeast. Some openly argued that political separation offered the most practical means of encouraging industrial development. One southerner, for instance, reasoned in 1860 that secession would stimulate direct trade with Europe and thereby help his region accumulate capital for mill building. "We think it rigidly demonstrable," he asserted, "that the ultimate result of disunion would be to give increased activity and impetus to every branch of Southern industry."[36]

Thus, as the sectional tension approached the breaking point in 1860, southerners who for years had preached the industrial gospel now hoped that their great opportunity was finally at hand. "Are we prepared for separate nationality?" William Gregg asked rhetorically. "It is absolutely necessary that we should make, within ourselves, all the prime necessaries of life, in order to secure independence."[37] Significantly, the goals of Gregg and his associates went far beyond the immediate military task. "Show Brother Jonathan that we have changed our tactics," Gregg cried out, "and that, in the future, we are to meet him in battle array—in the great field of commerce and home industry, where we intend to fight to the death against every attempt at usurpation."[38]

---

[34] Enoch Steadman, *The Southern Manufacturer: Showing the Advantage of Manufacturing Cotton in the Fields Where It Is Grown* (Gallatin, Tenn.: Gray and Boyers, 1858), pp. 100–101.

[35] J. M. Wesson to John F. H. Claiborne, August 11, 1858, Claiborne Papers, Southern Historical Collection, University of North Carolina, Chapel Hill.

[36] *De Bow's Review*, October 1860, p. 462.

[37] *De Bow's Review*, July 1860, pp. 78–80.

[38] *De Bow's Review*, December 1860, p. 772.

These prophets of the New South had clear ambitions for launching their own independent commercial empire. Leaders like Gregg, Hammond, and De Bow shared a world view, reinforced by their reading of history, that defined progress in terms of exporting finished goods and importing raw materials. De Bow repeated the familiar theme in an editorial prepared shortly before the firing on Fort Sumter. Throughout the ages, he maintained, advanced nations had grown in wealth and power by trading with backward countries which were "obliged to exchange large amounts of agricultural products for small amounts of mechanic and manufacturing products." After complaining that such an unequal connection made southerners "hewers of wood and drawers of water" for northerners, De Bow envisioned the rise of an industrial South benefiting from a similar relationship with the agrarian peoples of Latin America and Asia.[39]

It must be kept in mind, however, that most southerners who ultimately opted for disunion were not primarily concerned with industrial development and commercial expansion. Although sectional patriotism had helped to sustain interest in manufacturing, southerners never abandoned their traditional pattern of investing in land and slaves. What worried the dominant planter class most was the belief that the election of Abraham Lincoln in 1860 meant that slavery would be contained within its existing boundaries. Southerners also feared that the Republican coalition of eastern businessmen and western farmers would soon enact economic legislation inimical to their welfare. Feeling that time was running out, the planter elite decided to make a bid for separate nationhood.

During the war, the Confederate states made strenuous efforts to diversify their agriculture. The men in gray needed food, and the South could no longer depend upon the upper Mississippi Valley for grain and meat. After harvesting a bumper cotton crop in 1861, southerners quickly turned their attention to the cultivation of corn. Newspapers were filled with urgent appeals to grow provisions on the broad acres that had been devoted to the billowy white staple. "Plant Corn and Be Free," exclaimed a Georgia editor, "or plant cotton and be whipped." Where cotton or tobacco had

---

[39] *De Bow's Review*, May-June 1861, pp. 567–70.

already been started, many demanded that the crops be destroyed, either voluntarily by the planter or by his neighbors.[40]

But this question of how much land should be shifted from export commodities to cereals for home consumption soon became a matter of public policy rather than private decision. Patriotic meetings were held and leading southerners delivered fiery speeches condemning anyone who did not reduce his output of cotton and applauding planters who turned chiefly to corn. State governments even adopted legal measures to compel individual cooperation. The legislatures in Arkansas, Georgia, and South Carolina placed absolute limits upon cotton acreage; those in Alabama and Mississippi imposed a tax on production over a set amount. Sometimes dissenters took evasive action like raising grain along the highways and railroads while planting cotton well back where it could not be seen. Yet the tide of opinion favored provisions; and before the war ended, corn had become king in the mind of the South.[41]

The military struggle also heightened southern interest in manufacturing. Yankee products elicited hostility, and even agrarians with a short-range outlook understood the need for workshops to provide the rebel troops with munitions and uniforms. Veteran industrial boosters lost little time in seizing the chance to push for a balanced economy. They founded the Manufacturing and Direct Trade Association of the Confederate States soon after the fighting began.[42] As president of the organization, William Gregg repeatedly argued that a general system of manufacturing "must be brought into existence, or we will not long remain an independent people."[43] The Southern press likewise continued its cotton mill campaign behind the lines in the Confederacy. "If this war is to end in a resumption of old commercial relations with the Northern States," a Virginia editor declared, not atypically, "it might as well have never been fought."[44]

---

[40] Paul W. Gates, *Agriculture and the Civil War* (New York: Alfred A. Knopf, 1965), pp. 6–16.

[41] Ibid., pp. 17–19.

[42] E. Merton Coulter, *The Confederate States of America, 1861–1865* (Baton Rouge: Louisiana State University Press, 1950), pp. 211–12.

[43] Broadus Mitchell, *William Gregg: Factory Master of the Old South* (Chapel Hill: University of North Carolina Press, 1928), p. 230.

[44] *Richmond Daily Dispatch*, February 6, 1865.

Southern industrial crusaders welcomed the establishment of the federal blockade in 1861 as a blessing in disguise. The idea became prevalent that the closing of southern ports would act like the Embargo of 1807 in fostering manufacturing in Dixie. Newspapers published lists of new factories in an attempt to demonstrate that the blockade was aiding the South, and President Jefferson Davis boasted that "the injuries resulting from the interruptior of foreign commerce have received compensation by the development of our internal resources."[45] *De Bow's Review* agreed that the blockade "will make us very independent." The editor was confident that his section could achieve an integrated economy as a separate nation. "Let the South become one great workshop," he roared. "We shall beat the Yankees in time with their own tools."[46]

The Confederate States of America gave the cotton mill campaign official endorsement. Concerned with clothing the rebel army, the Confederate Congress passed exemption laws in 1862 excusing superintendents and operatives in wool and cotton manufacturing establishments from military service. The conscription act of 1864 abolished these exemptions, but it allowed for soldiers to be detailed for work in textile enterprises.[47] The Confederate government even altered its tariff schedule in an effort to stimulate home industry. Shortly after the war commenced, the Manufacturing and Direct Trade Association requested that textile machinery be placed on the free list. The Congress finally complied in 1863 by passing an act removing all duties on machinery used in wool and cotton factories.[48]

The war spirit, in short, had given rise to a widespread zeal for manufacturing in the Confederacy. Although skyrocketing prices provoked consumers to denounce industrialists along with almost everyone else as profiteers, the more discerning made a distinction between established businessmen and emergent speculators.[49] Pa-

---

[45] John C. Schwab, *The Confederate States of America, 1861–1865: A Financial and Industrial History of the South during the Civil War* (New Haven: Yale University Press, 1901), pp. 248–49.

[46] *De Bow's Review*, September 1861, pp. 329–30.

[47] Charles W. Ramsdell, "The Control of Manufacturing by the Confederate Government," *Mississippi Valley Historical Review* 8 (December 1921): 235–37; and Elizabeth Y. Webb, "Cotton Manufacturing and State Regulation in North Carolina, 1861–1865," *North Carolina Historical Review* 9 (April 1932): 129.

[48] Coulter, *The Confederate States of America*, p. 212.

[49] Ibid., pp. 219–32.

triotic southerners urged factory construction, and state legislatures granted numerous charters for new industrial projects. Yet shortages of capital, labor, and machinery permitted few of these enterprises to get into actual operation.[50] Southern foundries concentrated on war production, and the federal blockade hindered the importation of heavy equipment for the new mills. It was these material circumstances, and not theoretical principles, that prevented the Confederacy from entering into manufacturing on a more extensive scale.[51]

The battle for home industry continued beyond the antebellum period. Only the contestants had changed. Southerners were now striving to free themselves from economic peonage to New England rather than Old England. Though agriculture continued to outbid manufacturing for capital, the beginnings of a textile business had been established in the South. That accomplishment, while limited, did provide some southerners with valuable experience in factory management. More important for the future development of the section, a world view had emerged that regarded cotton manufacturing as a pioneer industry which required foreign markets to reach its full promise. Hence the foundations had been laid for the New South's quest for economic independence and commercial empire.

[50] Clement Eaton, *A History of the Southern Confederacy* (New York: Macmillan, 1954), p. 251.

[51] Charles W. Ramsdell, *Behind the Lines in the Southern Confederacy* (Baton Rouge: Louisiana State University Press, 1944), pp. 71–74.

Our Northern friends only deceive themselves when they think the South is to be for them in the future what it has been in the past.

Southern Recorder, 1865

The cultivation of cotton should be encouraged by all proper means, and should not be discouraged by onerous taxation.

New York Chamber of Commerce, 1866

I am frank enough to say that the people of my State, in my belief, are more interested in the removal of this tax than they are in any other question before the country. I am frank enough to say that the market of the South is as indispensable to our prosperity as our prosperity is necessary to our existence.

Senator William Sprague of Rhode Island, 1867

In the West we have a very large interest in stimulating the production of cotton. The southern States furnish the natural market to the Northwest for their great productions.

Senator Thomas A. Hendricks of Indiana, 1867

The West and the East and the North want purchasers. They want consumers for their manufactures and provisions. They want customers for their importations and freight for their ships. The South was the great consumer, the great purchaser, the great customer for the industry of the rest of the country.

National Intelligencer, 1868

In the present crippled and impoverished condition of the South, it is utterly impossible for her to produce a full cotton crop without the aid of Northern capital. She needs to be built up and restored to her former position of usefulness and commercial influence in the Union.

Boston Commercial Bulletin, 1868

2

The Business of Reconstruction

*R*ecent historical scholarship has tended to emphasize disunity in the American business community. Consistent with this trend, studies of the reconstruction era have pointed out that special interest groups in the North sharply divided in their response toward certain major economic issues confronting the war-torn nation.[1] Some Yankee entrepreneurs advocated high tariffs and hard money, while others favored low duties and soft currency. Differences such as these did exist. But on a deeper level northern business circles maintained a common attitude toward the conquered provinces. Although they engaged in many tactical debates regarding southern policy, they generally agreed upon the kind of commercial relationship that should prevail between the rebel states and the rest of the country. Thus a basic consensus underlay the conflicts involved in the business of reconstruction.

Southern cotton exports played a vital role in the functioning of the American economy in the years before the Civil War. Southerners exported more than half of their royal staple, and by 1860 King Cotton accounted for more than half the nation's total export trade. Large-scale cultivation in the Old South enabled the United States to pay for valuable capital goods imported from European countries with bales of cotton rather than bars of gold. Equally important, a large part of the revenue southerners received from the foreign sale of their great staple crop poured into other sections

[1] Robert P. Sharkey, *Money, Class, and Party: An Economic Study of the Civil War and Reconstruction* (Baltimore: Johns Hopkins University Press, 1959); and Stanley Coben, "Northeastern Business and Radical Reconstruction: A Reinterpretation," *Mississippi Valley Historical Review* 46 (June 1959): 67–90.

of the country in exchange for needed goods and services. The South purchased huge amounts of foodstuffs from the Northwest and manufactures from the Northeast. The South also sent vast quantities of money to New York and other mercantile centers along the eastern seaboard to pay insurance charges, warehouse fees, and shipping costs. In these ways, southern cotton exports lubricated both interregional and international flows of trade.[2]

Southerners frequently complained that their section suffered from the burdens of a colonial economy. Recent attempts by historians to discount the size of the southern market for western provisions have challenged the argument that southern wealth was largely transformed into northern profits. Yet while some states like Virginia and Maryland did ship wheat and flour out of the region, it must not be forgotten that the Deep South consumed a high percentage of the corn and pork raised in the upper Mississippi Valley.[3] The more significant historical problem, in any case, goes beyond making a mathematically precise computation of the southern trade. The crucial issue involves the way people at the time understood the relationship between the sections. The evidence here indicates that most leaders in the North believed that the South served as a valuable market for their farms as well as their factories. And this contemporary conviction was the operative historical reality that provided the context for the northern response to the secession crisis.

Northerners believed that the South's attempt to leave the Union threatened to sap the lifeblood of the American economy. If southerners succeeded in gaining their independence, the loss of foreign exchange derived from cotton exports would make it more difficult for the country to maintain a balance of payments. Disunion would in a similar manner undermine the prosperity of influential northern business groups. The Confederate aim to establish low tariffs and direct trade with Europe frightened eastern merchants and manufacturers. They were disturbed by nightmares of foreign vessels sailing into southern ports, unloading inexpensive industrial products duty free, and then taking on a full cargo of raw cotton for the return voyage across the Atlantic

---

[2] Douglass C. North, *The Economic Growth of the United States, 1790–1860* (New York: W. W. Norton, 1966).

[3] Diane L. Lindstrom, "Southern Dependence upon Interregional Grain Supplies: A Review of the Trade Flows, 1840–1860," *Agricultural History* 44 (January 1970): 110–13; and Paul W. Gates, *Agriculture and the Civil War* (New York: Alfred A. Knopf, 1965), pp. 9–10.

Ocean. Western farmers, at the same time, worried that the Confederacy would diversify its agriculture and perhaps even close the cheap Mississippi River route westerners used to reach overseas markets. Hence commercial interests throughout the North concluded that the economic consequences of secession would be intolerable.[4]

The Republican coalition of eastern businessmen and western agrarians, having calculated the value of the southern market, decided to wage war for the preservation of the Union. Then, after blocking the South's bid for separate nationhood, the major economic interest groups in the North stood determined to reap the benefits of their hard-won victory. The New York merchants eagerly awaited the opportunity to regain control of their profitable importing and exporting operations in the South. The Northwestern farmers and the Northeastern industrialists likewise looked forward to the resumption of their important southern sales. In short, these three key northern business interests were anxious to reconstruct the imperial relationship with the southern states which they had enjoyed during the antebellum period.

The controversy regarding economic reconstruction centered on the vitally important cotton question. The southern crop had suffered a drastic decline during the war, while cultivation correspondingly increased in Brazil, Egypt, and India. When the fighting ended, northern leaders realized that the revival of international and interregional trade flows depended upon the restoration of the southern staple to its commanding position in the world market. The victorious Yankees agreed on the need to stimulate cotton production in the vanquished section. But they debated among themselves the ways and means of securing the capital and labor required to accomplish their common objective.

The confusion and disruption brought about by the abolition of the peculiar institution gave rise to a serious labor problem in the South. Many northern capitalists feared that the emancipated slaves would refuse to go back to the plantations to serve as a cheap and tractable work force. Some hoped that white immigra-

---

[4] Kenneth M. Stampp, *And the War Came: The North and the Secession Crisis, 1860–1861* (Chicago: University of Chicago Press, 1965), pp. 123–27, 204–38; Philip S. Foner, *Business and Slavery: The New York Merchants and the Irrepressible Conflict* (Chapel Hill: University of North Carolina Press, 1941), pp. 12–13, and chap. 2; Robert G. Albion, *The Rise of the Port of New York, 1815–1860* (New York: Charles Scribner's Sons, 1939), chap. 6; and William A. Williams, *The Roots of the Modern American Empire* (New York: Random House, 1969), p. 101.

tion into the southern states would help overcome the difficulty, while others believed that it would be necessary to use force to get the blacks to return to the cotton fields. In the end, the freedmen were allowed to make their own choice: work or starve. Many former bondsmen took to the road at the first opportunity to express their freedom. But the economic whip soon brought most back to the reality of plantation life to toil as sharecroppers and tenant farmers.

The Freedmen's Bureau invoked the authority of the federal government to reinstate blacks to their traditional position in southern agriculture. Many of its wards refused to work for their old masters. Their resistance was reinforced by the widespread belief that their Yankee liberators would confiscate the large plantations and divide them into small plots for the use of the blacks. The government agency tried to disabuse the freedmen of their dreams of land ownership and persuade them to sign labor agreements with white proprietors. Bureau officials offered foodstuffs as an inducement for blacks to contract with planters and withheld provisions from those who continued idle in anticipation of receiving "forty acres and a mule." Some federal agents went beyond their instructions by cooperating with planters in forcing blacks back into field service. But the Freedmen's Bureau centered its policy on the liberal assumption that the market mechanism would solve the labor problem in the southern states. While it sought to condition blacks to respond to wage incentives rather than physical coercion, the basic aim remained unchanged. The black people would have to return to the cotton plantations so that the white staple could reassert its hold over the South.[5]

The question of who should supply the capital necessary to rejuvenate agriculture in the devastated region produced further divisions in northern business circles. The Boston Board of Trade

---

[5] Willie Lee Rose, *Rehearsal for Reconstruction: The Port Royal Story* (New York: Bobbs-Merrill, 1964); Joel Williamson, *After Slavery: The Negro in South Carolina during Reconstruction, 1861–1877* (Chapel Hill: University of North Carolina Press, 1965); Peter Kolchin, *First Freedom: The Response of Alabama's Blacks to Emancipation and Reconstruction* (Westport, Conn.: Greenwood Publishing, 1972); Roger Ransom and Richard Sutch, *One Kind of Freedom: The Economic Consequences of Emancipation* (New York: Cambridge University Press, 1977); James L. Roark, *Masters without Slaves: Southern Planters in the Civil War and Reconstruction* (New York: W. W. Norton, 1977); and Jonathan M. Wiener, *Social Origins of the New South: Alabama, 1860–1885* (Baton Rouge: Louisiana State University Press, 1978).

sponsored a grandiose scheme in late 1865 to expand the powers of the Freemen's Bureau to reorganize labor in the cotton states in order to "increase their production as nearly as possible to the quantity raised before the war." The project called for enormous outlays of government currency to purchase plantations and to supervise black field hands. But the New York Chamber of Commerce opposed the proposal. Though equally interested in promoting cotton planting, the merchants and bankers of the Empire State wanted to employ private capital rather than federal funds in underwriting the recolonization of the South.[6]

The New York mercantile community also registered strong objections to plans for using the former slaves for the purpose of building a wing of the Republican Party in the South. The masters of capital hastily reasoned that such political manipulation of the liberated blacks would create disorder in the southern states, discourage private investment in cotton culture, and delay the revival of southern agriculture. Nor did it take New England business leaders long to reach the same conclusion. The *Boston Post*, for example, announced in mid-1867 that the time had come to abandon political reconstruction. The editors complained that shortsighted politicians "keep out capital from the South, which would produce cotton there, and by destroying public confidence, prevent the growth of the one staple which is to restore at once their prosperity and that of the entire country."[7]

The New Englanders, moreover, soon joined the New Yorkers in extending financial support to southern cotton growers. The *Boston Commercial Bulletin* repeatedly appealed to northern capitalists to make liberal investments in the cotton states. "The renewed production, on the largest possible scale, of the great agricultural staples of the South," the editors explained in 1867, "is just the thing now wanted to build up Northern commerce, to enlarge the market for Northern manufactures, and give stability and soundness to the national currency, by keeping our supply of gold at home." The same journal pleaded with businessmen a few months later to loan money to the South and thereby "make her again a great producing region and a valuable ally to Northern commerce and manufactures." During the following year, these editors continued to argue that the South needed capital to be

---

[6] George R. Woolfolk, *The Cotton Regency: The Northern Merchants and Reconstruction, 1865–1880* (New York: Bookman Associates, 1958), pp. 48–60.

[7] *Boston Post*, as quoted in *Southern Recorder*, September 17, 1867.

"built up and restored to her former position of usefulness and commercial influence in the Union."[8]

The New England cotton manufacturers were especially concerned about conditions in the southern states. Already during the war, mill owners had expanded their productive capacity in preparation for future business. While many corporations took advantage of idle time to rebuild and enlarge their establishments, several new factories were constructed and put into operation. These farsighted entrepreneurs anticipated a period of great activity when hostilities ceased and southern cotton could be obtained again in large quantities.[9] The lords of the loom sought to regain their overseas trade that had been lost during the war. They also hoped to increase their home sales through the reconstruction of the rebel states and the recovery of their southern market.

The New England textile manufacturers, with an eye on expanding their domestic trade, stood firmly behind the protective tariff. The makers of knit goods even demanded higher duties for their recently established business. "If we get no increase," Amos A. Lawrence lamented, "then the manufacture must go back to Europe."[10] Most who did not produce specialties were content with the existing schedule, and many prominent mill owners like Edward Atkinson opposed increased rates. "The strongest men in the trade," Atkinson explained privately in 1866, "are more afraid of the unskilled competition built up at home by high duties than they are of foreign competition."[11] Some also feared that excessive rates would alienate western agrarians from the Republican Party. Yet the majority remained committed at least to a moderate tariff, and in 1868 they organized the National Association of Cotton Manufacturers in hopes of establishing a "bulwark against the enemies of the protective system."[12]

---

[8] *Boston Commercial Bulletin*, March 2, 1867; August 10, 1867; and June 6, 1868.

[9] Victor S. Clark, *History of Manufactures in the United States, 1860–1914*, 3 vols. (Washington, D.C.: Carnegie Institution of Washington, 1928), 2: 29.

[10] Amos A. Lawrence to David A. Wells, July 11, 1866, Lawrence Letterbook, Massachusetts Historical Society, Boston. See also Lawrence to Charles Sumner, January 25, 1867; and Lawrence to Wells, May 6, 1866.

[11] Edward Atkinson to Henry Wilson, July 9, 1866, Atkinson Letterbook, Massachusetts Historical Society, Boston. See also Atkinson to David A. Wells, July 11, 1866; Atkinson to Hugh McCulloch, May 28, 1867; and Lawrence to Wells, March 2, 1867, Lawrence Letterbook.

[12] Amos A. Lawrence to David S. Brown, May 29, 1868, Lawrence Letterbook.

The New England factory masters also agreed on the desirability of recapturing their foreign commerce. Their exports of rough cotton fabrics, particularly to China, had gradually increased during the antebellum period. Wartime shortages of raw cotton, however, sharply reduced the value of this business from more than ten million dollars in 1860 to under two million by 1864.[13] Great Britain lost little time in taking advantage of the situation. The failure of the American supply induced British spinners to adapt some of their machinery to manufacture Surat cotton, and the fabrication of this cheap Indian staple enabled them to strengthen their grip on the China market.

The New England manufacturers were eager to revive and extend their overseas trade. They quickly viewed the establishment of the United States Revenue Commission in 1865 under the leadership of David A. Wells in terms of marketplace expansion. Many wanted to raise revenue in the South in order to force the former rebels to help shoulder the war debt and to provide some relief for northern industries. Nearly everyone hoped for a reduction in the high taxes made necessary by the war. The removal of excise duties on coal, iron, and starch in particular would enable cotton manufacturers to lower their cost of production and thereby improve their position in the markets of the world.[14]

Representatives of the New England textile industry soon descended upon Washington to sponsor legislation designed to give them an advantage over their British rivals in foreign markets. Working closely with David A. Wells in the fall of 1865, the Boston lobby helped formulate a plan to tax raw cotton five cents a pound and to grant an equivalent drawback (i.e., rebate) on exports of the manufactured fiber.[15] They confidently assumed that the American crop would rule the world market and that the European spinners would be compelled to pay the tax. Then the drawback would empower New England "to compete, on a very large scale, for the business of supplying the world with manufactured goods." Even those who feared that the English would continue to use the untaxed Indian staple to produce coarse goods believed that the kick-

---

[13] U.S., Department of Commerce and Labor, *Statistical Abstract of the United States, 1910*, p. 491.

[14] U.S., Congress, House, *Executive Document* No. 34, 39th Cong., 1st sess., 1866. See Appendix to Special Report No. 3.

[15] Herbert R. Ferleger, *David A. Wells and the American Revenue System, 1865–1870* (New York: Columbia University Libraries, 1942), pp. 59–61.

back would enable the Boston mill owners to supplant Britain in the China market.[16]

The New York business community, having everything to lose and nothing to gain, opposed the New England strategy from the outset. Merchants in the imperial city feared that a high tax would delay the return of American primacy in the international cotton market and thereby interfere with the restoration of their profitable southern trade. The *New York Commercial and Financial Chronicle* warned again and again that competition in foreign countries had increased during the war and that nothing should be done to retard southern production.[17] The New York Chamber of Commerce agreed, and in May 1866 it dispatched a strong memorial against the proposed measure. "The cultivation of cotton should be encouraged by all proper means," the association declared unanimously, "and should not be discouraged by onerous taxation."[18]

By the spring of 1866, even the New England manufacturers had lost their earlier optimism about the ability of the southern crop to regain its hegemony in the world market.[19] "As the old cotton keeps coming and the prospects of the new crop improve," Atkinson advised Wells on April 11, "it becomes evident that the world will have a surplus of cotton much sooner than we thought last summer. When there is a surplus the untaxed product regulates the price and the taxed product will pile up."[20] The next day, Atkinson persuaded several leading industrialists to petition Justin S. Morrill, Chairman of the House Ways and Means Committee, against any excise higher than three cents a pound.[21] The New Yorkers still objected, but Congress followed Boston's desires and passed an act in July 1866 providing for a three cent tax on raw cotton and an equal drawback on manufactured exports.

Meanwhile, as Yankee business interests tried to reestablish

---

[16] U.S., Congress, House, *Executive Document* No. 34, 1866. See Appendix to Special Report No. 3.

[17] *New York Commercial and Financial Chronicle*, November 25, 1865, pp. 674–75; February 17, 1866, pp. 195–97; March 24, 1866, pp. 354–55; May 5, 1866, p. 546; and June 23, 1866, p. 770.

[18] U.S., Congress, Senate, *Miscellaneous Document* No. 109, 39th Cong., 1st sess., 1866.

[19] Fergler, *David A. Wells*, pp. 84–85; and Woolfolk, *The Cotton Regency*, p. 62.

[20] Edward Atkinson to David A. Wells, April 11, 1866, Atkinson Letterbook.

[21] Memorial to J. S. Morrill, April 12, 1866, Atkinson Letterbook.

their advantageous connection with the defeated section, the former rebels rekindled antebellum dreams of freeing themselves
from the fetters of a colonial economy. Southerners were determined to diversify their agriculture by reducing the number of
acres devoted to cotton and by producing more grain and meat.
They were equally intent on repairing worn factories and expanding their industrial base. These ambitions, in fact, prompted the
great majority of articulate southerners to renew their drive to
achieve sectional economic independence.

Southern leaders launched a vigorous cotton mill campaign
shortly after surrendering at Appomattox. While the abolition of
slavery provoked fears that cotton cultivation would no longer
yield profitable returns, the operation of textile factories promised
to reward investors with liberal dividends. Spinning and weaving
mills would also provide employment for widows, orphans, and
other war victims and thereby remove the burden of support from
the state. Southerners regarded cotton manufacturing as a pioneer
industry that would pave the way for related enterprises. They
believed that the rise of urban centers would in turn create local
markets for farm produce and make them less dependent upon
cotton culture. Almost everyone agreed that cotton mill building
would spark general economic development and restore prosperity
and power to the entire region.

Newspapers throughout the southern states bristled with appeals to bring the cotton factories to the cotton fields. "Cotton will
be the regenerator of our impoverished South," declared the *Daily
Columbus Enquirer.* "But it must not only be produced, but manufactured at home."[22] *De Bow's Review* likewise regarded the erection of textile establishments as imperative: *"We have got to go to
manufacturing to save ourselves."*[23] The *Macon Telegraph* predicted
that emancipation would "throw investments out of the old ruts"
and that cotton manufacturing would become "a leading interest
in the South."[24] And the *Jackson Clarion* commended those planters who were "turning their attention to manufacturing at home
our own raw staple, instead of sending it North to be manufactured by our bitterest enemies, and then returned to us at the most
fabulous prices."[25]

[22] *Daily Columbus Enquirer,* June 3, 1866.
[23] *De Bow's Review,* February 1867, pp. 172–78. (Emphasis in the original.)
[24] *Macon Telegraph,* as quoted in *Southern Recorder,* October 6, 1868.
[25] *Jackson Clarion,* as quoted in *De Bow's Review,* March 1867, p. 312.

The cotton tax, imposed by the Republican Congress, gave added impetus to the southern mill fever. Already bitter about the war and black reconstruction, southerners viewed the excise as an unjust discrimination that singled out the agricultural producers in their section for special punishment. They also charged that the levy violated the constitutional prohibition against export duties since most of the crop was sold abroad. Worse yet, many southerners feared that their leading staple would meet stiff competition in the international market and that the tax would turn European factories to the fields of India, Egypt, and Brazil, thereby striking a severe blow to their own economy. This apprehension reinforced southern aspirations to manufacture their cotton crop before shipping it overseas.

So did the procedure established for implementing the tax. The southern states were divided into several districts for the purpose of gathering the revenue, but the assessment did not become collectable until the staple was transported to outlying areas. Hence southerners could escape payment by manufacturing their own cotton within the tax districts where it was grown, while the drawback on exported textiles promised to enhance their competitive position in foreign markets. Industrial crusaders quickly advised their listeners to take advantage of the situation. The *New Orleans Picayune*, for instance, urged southerners to erect cotton mills inside the tax districts to exploit the opportunity at hand. The *Columbus Sun* approved the idea: "Let us make hay while the sun shines."[26]

Even while Congress was debating the tax, the president of Emory College called for the construction of cotton factories to counteract the measure. He warned that southerners should "anticipate unequal sectional legislation, with heavy discrimination against our great staples, and in favor of Northern industry." But, he continued, "because we have been vanquished in a trial of arms, we need not therefore abandon all hope of defense." He then pleaded with southerners to manufacture cotton for home and export markets. "That policy alone offers the hope of a refuge from oppression, and eternal subserviency to our Northern neighbors."[27] The *Daily Columbus Enquirer* was in complete agreement. "Do this

---

[26] *New Orleans Picayune* and *Columbus Sun*, as quoted in *Southern Recorder*, October 2, 1866.

[27] *Scott's Monthly Magazine*, June 1866, pp. 486–95.

and the Northern States will drop the export duty like a red hot bar of iron, or, holding on to it, will only burn their own hands," the editors cried. "Do it not, and ruin STARES US IN THE FACE!"[28]

The cotton tax provoked more and more people in the South to reflect upon the wisdom of expanding their textile industry. "All concur in its importance," the *Charleston Courier* reported. "True prosperity consists in not only raising, but in commencing to manufacture all that we can within ourselves," the editors reasoned. "It will confer more power than that of mere politics, and will in time create a real and substantial independence."[29] Likewise convinced that the tax had encouraged cotton mill building, the *Southern Recorder* hoped that it would remain on the books. "We are but one among many thousands," the editors noted, "that hold this opinion and speak for the permanent good of the whole South."[30]

Anticipating southern rivalry, some New England textile spokesmen by contrast began agitating for the abolition of the excise on cotton. "The existing tax drives the South into directly manufacturing for itself," the *Boston Post* warned. "It likewise diverts its industry into more profitable channels, thus creating the variety which will soon enough betray its effects in the industrial independence of its people. That will be well for that section, but it is a prosperity gained by suddenly withering our own." The editors hoped that the levy would be annulled in order to restore the old colonial pattern when "the South produced cotton; the West grain and meat; and the East manufactured goods, in large part from the very cotton it bought from the South."[31]

Most New England cotton manufacturers, however, were concerned more about losing their southern market than about the rise of harmful industrial competition in the devastated region. Shortly after the excise passed, Edward Atkinson warned David A. Wells that "by December 1867 the entire removal of the cotton tax will be necessary."[32] It was becoming increasingly apparent that the levy would discourage cotton cultivation and leave southerners without the means to purchase northern goods. The Boston Board of Trade, therefore, sent two men to Washington in February

---

[28] *Daily Columbus Enquirer,* June 2, 1866.

[29] *Charleston Courier,* October 17, 1866.

[30] *Southern Recorder,* December 24, 1867.

[31] *Boston Post,* as quoted in *De Bow's Review,* July-August 1867, p. 111.

[32] Atkinson to Wells, November 22, 1866, Atkinson Letterbook.

1867 to lobby against the destructive measure.[33] Aided by strong representation in the Senate, the New Englanders were able in March to get the tax reduced a half cent.

Never wavering from their original stand, the New York business community participated in this growing movement to repeal the cotton tax. "Our trade is prostrate," complained Representative Demas Barnes, himself a New York merchant. "The curse of our tax, like chickens, has come home to roost. We of the North share in the desolation of the southern states."[34] In New York the *Commercial and Financial Chronicle* argued again and again in 1867 that the excise on cotton would impoverish the southern provinces and destroy their commercial value to the rest of the country.[35] Agitation against the tax continued, and by December the Republican Congress once again turned its attention to the crucial cotton question.

New England senators candidly explained their chief reason for demanding the abolition of the tax. "Cotton is no longer king," thundered Henry Wilson of Massachusetts. He wanted the excise removed to encourage cotton production so that southerners could buy northern commodities.[36] "If we want to sell northern manufactures at the South," James W. Patterson of New Hampshire agreed, "we must give to the southern people something to purchase with."[37] William Sprague of Rhode Island, himself one of the largest cotton manufacturers in the country, made the same analysis: "I am frank enough to say that the people of my State, in my belief, are more interested in the removal of this tax than they are in any other questions before the country. I am frank enough to say that the market of the South is as indispensable to our prosperity as our prosperity is necessary to our existence."[38]

Northwestern senators were equally open in their denunciations of the tax. "I do not think it good policy to drive the South into the culture of new products," John Sherman of Ohio declared.

---

[33] Woolfolk, *The Cotton Regency*, pp. 84–85.

[34] U.S., Congress, House, *Congressional Globe*, 40th Cong., 2nd sess., December 3, 1867, 39, pt. 1: 16.

[35] *New York Commercial and Financial Chronicle*, August 3, 1867, pp. 135–36; October 12, 1867, pp. 455–56; and December 28, 1867, pp. 807–8.

[36] U.S., Congress, Senate, *Congressional Globe*, 40th Cong., 2nd sess., December 16, 1867, 39, pt. 1: 203–5.

[37] Ibid., January 7, 1868, pp. 348–49.

[38] Ibid., December 20, 1867, p. 304.

"Perhaps I speak in an interested point of view; for we are interested. The State of Ohio, like the State of Illinois, furnishes a large quantity of food which goes into the production of this cotton."[39] Many others repeated the argument. "In the West I think we have a very large interest in stimulating the production of cotton," Thomas A. Hendricks of Indiana explained. "The southern States furnish the natural market to the Northwest for their great productions."[40] James W. Grimes of Iowa concurred. "We want the southern States to furnish in the future as they once did," he concluded, "a reliable market for the agricultural products of the Northwest."[41]

Many government officials threw their weight against the excise on cotton for broader reasons. The United States Commissioners to the Paris Exposition warned in August 1867 that the southern crop could not regain its preeminence in the world market unless the tax was removed. They wanted its production increased because cotton was "the chief export of the country in adjusting balances of trade and exchanges."[42] Secretary of Treasury Hugh McCulloch, in his December annual report, likewise regarded cotton exports as vital to the entire economic system. "The great staples of the South have for many years constituted a large portion of our exports," he pointed out, adding that they had saved America from ruinous indebtedness to Europe during the past year. "It is of the greatest moment," McCulloch concluded, "that the productive power of the Southern States should be restored as rapidly as possible."[43]

These economic considerations ultimately led in February 1868 to the complete removal of the cotton tax. The measure threatened to disrupt America's foreign trade and cause a drain of specie from the national Treasury. It also presented a menace to commercial intercourse between the different sections of the country. Northwestern farmers and Northeastern manufacturers, therefore, joined hands with New York merchants to get the tax abolished in order to restore the old colonial arrangement. "The West and the

---

[39] Ibid., p. 300.

[40] Ibid., December 17, 1867, p. 227.

[41] Ibid., December 20, 1867, p. 303.

[42] U.S., Congress, Senate, Commissioners to the Paris Exposition, *Report upon Cotton*, 40th Cong., 2nd sess., 1867, p. 7. The report was written by E. R. Mudge, a New England manufacturer.

[43] *Southern Recorder*, December 17, 1867.

East and the North want purchasers," the *National Intelligencer* explained in summary. "They want consumers for their manufactures and provisions. They want customers for their importations and freight for their ships. The South was the great consumer, the great purchaser, the great customer for the industry of the rest of the country."[44]

Northerners withdrew the tax to help King Cotton reassert its dominion over the international market. At the same time, they poured large amounts of money into the South to facilitate the growth of the much desired fiber. Their goals were soon achieved. A supplementary report of the Commissioners to the Paris Exposition announced in 1869 that the southern states were "rapidly regaining the position held before the war," adding that the abolition of the tax had assured "the restoration of their monopoly of the cotton supply of the world."[45] As a result, agricultural diversification was discouraged and the South remained under the curse of a colonial economy.

The southern press, however, continued to battle against a single crop system. "Our Northern friends only deceive themselves when they think the South is to be for them in the future what it has been in the past," the *Southern Recorder* proclaimed in response to Yankee attempts to promote cotton production.[46] "In common with our contemporaries all over the South," exhorted the *New Orleans Price-Current*, "we urge upon the planters not only to diversify their crops but to make strenuous efforts in the way of stock raising so as to place themselves completely independent of other sections of the country in respect to both meats and cereals."[47] Despite such pleas, the lure of high cotton prices immediately following the war induced many farmers trying to eke out an existence in the impoverished region to return to old habits of cultivation.

Thus, together with this decision of southern agrarians, the policy pursued by northern leaders helped perpetuate the colonial status of the South. Yankee economic interests had done everything in their power during the postwar years to renew their im-

---

[44] *National Intelligencer*, as quoted in *Southern Recorder*, January 28, 1868.

[45] U.S., Congress, Senate, Commissioners to the Paris Exposition, *Supplementary Report upon Cotton*, 40th Cong., 2nd sess., p. 10. The report was written in 1869 by B. F. Nourse, a New England manufacturer.

[46] *Southern Recorder*, August 29, 1865.

[47] *New Orleans Price-Current*, December 22, 1869.

perial relationship with the rebel states. Their efforts focused on stimulating cotton production in order to restore the antebellum pattern of international and interregional commerce. Though they often disagreed over the means needed to attain their basic objective, northern merchants, manufacturers, and farmers maintained a common desire to exploit the southern states. And it was this consensus in the North that determined the fundamental approach to the business of reconstruction.

There is much reason to hope that the late slave States, relying on their internal resources, will achieve an independence almost as much to be desired as that which would have resulted from a separate government.

A Southern Literary Magazine, 1866

We are going to work in good earnest, not only to repair the waste places of war, but to build up and improve and prosper, and to show to the world that we can be as good soldiers in peace as we are in war, and that we intend to achieve some most glorious victories on the fields of labor and in the chambers of commerce.

A Mississippi Cotton Mill Crusader, 1866

The wager of battle decided against us, and there is no appeal from the decision, but there is yet another struggle we can make.

A Mississippi College Professor, 1870

The conflict between New England and the South as the true seat of cotton manufacture has just fairly begun.

Henry Grady, *Atlanta Constitution*, 1881

If Eastern men get rates reduced we can get rates reduced also. We can whip them any way they want to fight.

A Southern Cotton Manufacturer, 1883

I still draw a grain of comfort from the present cotton goods depression. In this struggle caused by overproduction the fittest must survive.

An Augusta Textile Executive, 1884

3

The New South's Struggle for Economic Independence

Standard accounts of the New South era have been based upon the assumption that industrialism and nationalism were integrated in southern thinking.[1] Spokesmen for manufacturing are portrayed as repentant rebels who had renounced their feelings of sectional animosity and who looked forward to engaging in economic cooperation with their military conquerors. It is true that the vanquished people accepted the fact that their quest for separate nationhood had been crushed by northern armies and that their bid for industrial development would have to be made within the political framework of the Union. Yet a closer examination of the movement to bring the cotton factories to the cotton fields indicates that southerners sought revenge rather than reconciliation.

The military ordeal provided the psychological backdrop for the New South's campaign to achieve economic independence during the last third of the nineteenth century. Yankee raiders

---

[1] Broadus Mitchell, *The Rise of Cotton Mills in the South* (Baltimore: Johns Hopkins University Press, 1921); Paul H. Buck, *The Road to Reunion, 1865–1900* (Baltimore: Little, Brown and Co., 1937). For an updated version of the traditional interpretation, see Paul M. Gaston, *The New South Creed: A Study in Southern Myth-Making* (Baton Rouge: Louisiana State University Press, 1970). Following the lead of Mitchell and Buck, Gaston links the rise of southern industry to the decline in sectional hostility: "The announcement of the death of sectionalism in the South was present in virtually every discussion of the New South movement" (p. 91). For a much-neglected view contrary to the standard account, see W. J. Cash, *The Mind of the South* (New York: Random House, 1941). Cash likened the erection of cotton factories in the New South to taking a "new charge at Gettysburg" (p. 188).

demolished railroads, burned factories and barns, stole horses and mules, and wrecked farm implements. Hundreds of thousands of Confederate troops died while defending their homeland, and many more lost an eye or limb or received some other injury that crippled them for life. Few southern families escaped from the scourge of death and destruction. These wartime experiences, combined with the humiliation of defeat, produced a deep desire to retaliate against the triumphant North.

Southern advocates of a new order in the years following the Civil War did not give up the fight against their old enemies. They constantly complained that their region suffered from the burdens of a colonial economy; and they made a concerted effort to diversify their agriculture and expand their industrial base in order to curb the drain of their wealth to pay for manufactures and foodstuffs imported from other parts of the country. The tremendous waste and impoverishment resulting from the war spurred almost everyone in the South to support the drive to transform their region from a captive customer into a formidable competitor of their northern foes. The crusade to improve material conditions in the postbellum South thus moved the sectional conflict from the military arena to the economic battlefield.

The New South's program for economic development centered on a sustained struggle to establish a large-scale textile business. Southerners regarded cotton manufacturing as a leading sector industry which would enable them to overhaul their entire economy. The introduction of spinning and weaving factories would offer work for unemployed whites and reward investers with handsome dividends. As profits were plowed back into the mills, the burgeoning textile business would attract machine shops and related enterprises. Other industries would then move south, giving added value to real estate. More important, the growth in urban population would stimulate diversified farming by increasing the local demand for meat and grain.

The southern states possessed an excellent combination of resources for cotton manufacturing. Broad fields covered with the white staple provided an unlimited quantity of raw material which could be transported to the nearby mills at little cost. The mountain streams flowing down to the sea afforded abundant water power to run the machinery. Finally, the lower class whites who lived in the neighboring countryside furnished a large supply of cheap and tractable labor. Southerners were anxious to exploit these advantages. Thus, shortly after surrendering in 1865, they launched an aggressive cotton mill campaign in an attempt to overcome their colonial status and subdue their conqueror with his own weapons.

Southerners resented the emancipation of their slaves, but they found comfort in the belief that abolition would encourage investment in manufacturing in their region and thereby undermine the North's industrial supremacy. The *Southern Recorder,* for example, predicted spitefully in 1865 that northerners "will yet find out to their sorrow that the destruction of our negro property has laid the foundation for an independence that will strike fatal blows at their prosperity." During the antebellum period, the editors explained, a basic "community of interests" prevailed as the North exchanged its finished products for the South's raw materials. But now that southerners intended to reform their own economy "competition, jealousies, and rivalship" would mark the future relations between the two sections. The editors confidently concluded that the New South would "beat the brains out of New England with the club she has so foolishly put into our hands."[2]

The war analogies that punctuated the rhetoric of New South proponents illustrate their strong determination to strike back at the North. One Mississippian articulated the predominant sentiment in his section when he urged planters to manufacture their own cotton in order to turn the military defeat into an economic victory. "We are going to work in good earnest, not only to repair the waste places of war, but to build up and improve and prosper," he announced in 1866, "and to show to the world that we can be as good soldiers in peace as we are in war, and that we intend to achieve some most glorious victories on the fields of labor and in the chambers of commerce."[3] The *Montgomery Mail* similarly boasted that the construction of cotton factories in the southern states would "shake to pieces the artificial power of our enemies."[4]

Southerners continued to take pleasure in the idea that their own economic improvement would come at the expense of their northern neighbors. "The Southern people were the great customers of their wares," noted the *Southern Recorder* in 1868. "But with the destruction of their slave property Yankee wealth will diminish year by year, as the South comes into the market as an active and determined competitor against them in their own busi-

---

[2] *Southern Recorder,* November 28, 1865.

[3] William J. Barbee, *The Cotton Question* (New York: Metropolitan Record Office, 1866), pp. 138–42.

[4] *Montgomery Mail,* as quoted in *Daily Columbus Enquirer,* October 4, 1866.

ness."[5] The *Savannah Republican* likewise looked ahead to the time when the southern states would become the center of cotton manufacturing in the country. "What a glorious day that will be for the South," the editors gloated in 1869, "and how completely she will be avenged upon her enemies in New England, who have sought to humiliate and destroy her."[6] A professor at the University of Mississippi expressed the same notion a year later. "The wager of battle decided against us, and there is no appeal from the decision," he lectured, "but there is yet another struggle we can make." Let the South establish a broad factory system and she will grow in prosperity and power "until her conqueror will sink slowly into her train-bearer."[7]

Old-time industrial promoters like William Gregg of South Carolina led the charge against the northern enemy. His famous factory at Graniteville had supplied large amounts of cloth to the rebel army; and soon after the Confederacy capitulated, Gregg sailed for Europe to purchase new machinery to replace worn equipment and expand operations. While he gathered these implements of economic warfare, news from home announcing the birth of a grandson prompted him to communicate his hostility for the North as he reflected upon the boy's future. "You must not send him to any Yankee College," Gregg wrote back. "He must be brought up in the faith of a true southerner and a Reb every inch of him."[8] Gregg hoped that the financial success of the Graniteville company would inspire southerners to pool whatever money they could spare to build cotton mills. He feared that without such establishments "our beloved South will be to the balance of the Union what Ireland has been and is to England."[9]

Southern newspapers and business journals also clamored for home industry to break the chains of a colonial economy. "To be prosperous, and independent, it is not alone necessary to till the soil," the New Orleans *Price-Current* exhorted in 1865. "We must have manufactories that will supply us with machinery and every

[5] *Southern Recorder*, April 14, 1868.

[6] *Savannah Republican*, as quoted in *De Bow's Review*, December 1869, p. 1075.

[7] *XIX Century*, February 1870, p. 686.

[8] William Gregg to Clara Chaffee, July 14, 1866, Gregg Papers, Library of Congress, Washington, D.C.

[9] Broadus Mitchell, *William Gregg, Factory Master of the Old South* (Chapel Hill: University of North Carolina Press, 1928), p. 245.

description of manufactured goods that our condition requires."[10]
Several articles appearing in *De Bow's Review* during the following
year stressed the same self-sufficiency theme. "To the North we
have been hewers of wood and drawers of water," one writer lamented in the contemporary way of describing the phenomenon of
internal imperialism. "The cotton crop will be soon on hand," he
continued. "Instead of spending at the North every cent realized
from it, would it not be much better to make many articles of
consumption at home and enrich our own people?"[11]

Even southern literary periodicals participated in the crusade
for sectional economic independence. "The mistaken policy of the
past is now painfully realized by our people," *Scott's Monthly Magazine* proclaimed in 1866. "They are awakened to a lively sense of
the heavy tribute which they foolishly paid to other sections, in
their wanton disregard of the advantages at their command." The
editors predicted that the rise of cotton mills and other business
concerns would give the South "an independence almost as much
to be desired as that which would have resulted from a separate
government."[12] With the same objective in mind, *The Land We Love*
called for a sweeping reform in southern education. "We must
abandon the aesthetic and the ornamental for the practical and
the useful," the editors insisted in 1866, explaining that while the
old curriculum had produced statesmen and orators, "we became
dependent upon the North for everything."[13]

This widespread enthusiasm for cotton manufacturing did produce some tangible results despite the severe capital shortage in
the immediate postwar years. Southerners repaired ruined factories, increased the capacity of others, and built new ones. The hum
of spindles and looms running in Alabama, Georgia, and the Carolinas generated a sense of confidence; and many new ventures
were projected. But the depression between 1873 and 1878 retarded the movement for industrial expansion. Plans for the erection of new textile establishments were shelved, and many
enterprises already under construction remained unfinished for
several years. Hence, at the end of the depression, the South had

---

[10] *New Orleans Price-Current*, November 29, 1865.

[11] *De Bow's Review*, September 1866, p. 286.

[12] *Scott's Monthly Magazine*, June 1866, pp. 505–7.

[13] *The Land We Love*, May 1866, pp. 1–11.

only about a half million active cotton spindles compared with over eight million in New England.[14]

The upswing in the business cycle beginning in 1879, however, gave a renewed impetus to the movement to bring the cotton factories to the cotton fields. Small town and city newspapers throughout the southern states were filled with pleas for cotton manufacturing to promote general economic development and consequently provide relief from the ills of a one crop system. The *Atlanta Constitution* assured its readers in 1880 that the establishment of textile plants would "bring a long train of other factories and shops and agencies to furnish supplies."[15] Trumpeting the standard argument a year later, the *Carolina Spartan* reasoned that the growing number of workers in a nearby mill village would encourage agricultural diversification. "These people must be fed," the editors pointed out, "and whatever of a marketable character the farmers will bring to the place can be sold."[16]

The mounting agitation sparked a dramatic cotton mill boom in the South during the prosperous period between 1879 and 1883. A great number of new textile firms were organized, and many already established companies expanded their operations. The major part of the activity took place in the piedmont region in the South Atlantic states. South Carolina more than tripled its cotton spindle capacity during these years of swift growth.[17] Georgia also made significant gains; the city of Augusta alone added 63,000 new spindles.[18] Alabama and North Carolina experienced a similar development. As a result, the New South finally began to challenge New England in the contest for supremacy in cotton manufacturing.

Southerners themselves were primarily responsible for the rapid expansion of their textile industry.[19] The smaller undertak-

---

[14] U.S., Department of Interior, *Twelfth Census of the United States*, 1900, Manufactures, 9, pt. 3: 54–57.

[15] *Atlanta Constitution*, December 4, 1880.

[16] *Carolina Spartan*, July 27, 1881.

[17] James R. Young, *Textile Leaders of the South* (Columbia, S.C.: R. L. Bryan Co., 1963), p. 509.

[18] Mitchell, *The Rise of Cotton Mills in the South*, p. 71.

[19] Jack Blicksilver, *Cotton Manufacturing in the Southeast: An Historical Analysis* (Atlanta: Bureau of Business and Economic Research, Georgia State College of Business Administration, Bulletin No. 5, July 1959), pp. 5–6; Holland Thompson, *From the Cotton Field to the Cotton Mill: A Study in Industrial Transition in North Carolina* (New York: Macmillan Co., 1906), p. 81; and Andrew W. Pierpont, "Development of the Textile Industry in Alamance County, North Carolina" (Ph.D. dissertation, University of North Carolina, 1953), p. 174.

ings depended almost exclusively upon the financial backing of local town dwellers and residents of the surrounding countryside. The wide variety of stockholders included farmers and planters, as well as doctors, lawyers, and clergymen. Most of the funds that gave rise to the larger establishments also came from native sources, particularly from businessmen in the leading southern cities. Charleston merchants and jobbers invested heavily in the impressive factories which sprang up in the South Carolina backcountry. Atlanta bankers and brokers in like manner interested themselves in some of the big enterprises organized in Georgia.

Two northern business groups, however, did help these southern industrial promoters solve their financial problems. New England machine makers extended liberal credits to new ventures, and intense competition for the southern market eventually led some firms to accept mill stock as partial payment for equipment. New York and Boston commission houses often supplied working capital for southern factories, and a few also took shares in return for the privilege of marketing the goods produced. Yet the amount of outside investment should not be overestimated. While the Lowell Machine Shop and the Whitin Machine Works dominated southern sales, the former absolutely refused to accept any stock and the latter took very little.[20] Most other equipment companies who did subscribe sold their shares back to southerners as soon as possible. Though the commission houses generally retained their ownership, they usually invested even less in southern textile enterprises than the machine makers.[21]

Northern capitalists instead funnelled large sums of money into extractive industries like mining and lumbering which drew raw materials from the South for processing outside the region. They likewise extended railroad lines into the southern states to exploit their minerals and forests as well as to open markets for Yankee merchandise. But northerners did not invest heavily in developmental industries which would compete with their own business interests. Thus the emergence of the southern iron industry followed the same pattern already established in cotton manufacturing. Southerners primarily depended upon their own

---

[20] George S. Gibb, *The Saco-Lowell Shops: Textile Machine Building in New England, 1813–1949* (Cambridge: Harvard University Press, 1950), pp. 244–46; and Thomas R. Navin, *The Whitin Machine Works since 1831* (Cambridge: Harvard University Press, 1950), pp. 229–30.

[21] Blicksilver, *Cotton Manufacturing in the Southeast*, p. 8; and Mitchell, *The Rise of Cotton Mills in the South*, pp. 242–47.

capital in launching the Alabama iron industry in the 1880s, and southern inroads into the national metal market soon worried Pittsburgh ironmasters. Andrew Carnegie, after investigating the Birmingham district in 1889, declared that "the South is Pennsylvania's most formidable industrial enemy." Northerners ultimately used their financial power to buy out their major southern rivals. Then they imposed a pricing policy designed to retard iron and steel development in Dixie.[22]

Southerners, in the meantime, continued to direct their cotton mill campaign against their northern conquerors. Bitter recollections of the war still aroused people in the defeated section, and their economic accomplishments elicited feelings of sweet revenge. The vanquished rebels hailed the erection of each new cotton factory as a victory over the hated Yankee. The *Columbus Enquirer* reflected the general sentiment while pointing with pride to Georgia's growing number of cotton spindles. "These are the weapons peace gave us," cried the editors in 1880, "and right trusty ones they are."[23] A year later, Henry Grady's *Atlanta Constitution* declared that "the conflict between New England and the South as the true seat of cotton manufacture has just fairly begun." The paper was confident that despite their lack of capital and experience the southern states would ultimately win the battle.[24]

Southerners reacted angrily to New England suggestions that

---

[22] Jonathan M. Wiener, *Social Origins of the New South: Alabama, 1860–1885* (Baton Rouge: Louisiana State University Press, 1978), pp. 168–83. Wiener nicely summarizes the Birmingham case: "When outside capital finally was obtained by Birmingham developers, around 1880, it came not from the centers of finance in New York, Boston, and Philadelphia, but from the periphery, from Nashville and Cincinnati and Louisville, from the second and third string of industrialists and financiers. Northeastern capitalists first refused to invest in mines and blast furnaces as the mineral region was being opened; then they refused to support the technological innovations in coking coal that could make the region a major pig iron center. Once the pig iron was in production, they failed to invest in conversion to steel; once the technology of making basic pig iron good enough for steel was perfected, the northeastern interests bought the iron for their own manufacturing, further delaying the development of southern steelmaking capacity; and, when Birmingham had at last converted to steel, northeastern capital finally bought in, but with the purpose of holding back southern steel production, retarding the growth of southern manufactured goods which competed with their own" (p. 183).

[23] *Columbus Enquirer*, as quoted in *Atlanta Constitution*, March 9, 1880.

[24] *Atlanta Constitution*, January 21, 1881.

they should remain on the agricultural half of an imperial relationship with the industrial North. They were especially incensed when Edward Atkinson, a prominent Boston textile executive, traveled to Atlanta in 1880 and amid great fanfare advised southerners to leave the manufacturing end of the cotton business to northerners.[25] The southern press immediately turned Atkinson into a symbol of Yankee oppression, and editorials for the next twenty years ridiculed him as they saluted the rise of cotton factories in their section. Southerners were equally enraged by the attempts of New England mill owners to obtain railway concessions as a device to foil their industrial crusade. "If Eastern men get rates reduced we can get rates reduced," a member of the Southern Manufacturers' Association proclaimed in 1883. "We can whip them any way they want to fight."[26]

The southern counterattack also involved an intense campaign against the tariff on textile machinery. High charges on imports made from iron and steel increased the expense of mill building and thereby hindered economic development in areas possessing little capital. Southern senators and representatives took every opportunity to call for the repeal of all duties on textile equipment. They introduced bills, offered amendments, and presented resolutions urging the abolition of the measure. Congressman Emory L. Speer of Georgia in 1881 summarized the case against the levy on machinery imported from abroad. He concluded his argument with a simple demand—"We want the load taken off."[27]

Southern agitation swelled in 1883 when New England political leaders, after consulting with influential cotton manufacturers, proposed a hike in the tariff on textile equipment.[28] Newspapers in the major southern cities like Atlanta, Charleston, Memphis, and New Orleans loudly denounced the northern scheme. Agricultural periodicals in the South were just as vocal in their dissent. "Nothing could be more outrageous," shouted the Planters' Journal. "Instead of the duty on cotton machinery being increased, it should

[25] See, for example, Augusta Chronicle and Constitutionalist, October 23, 1880; Huntsville Weekly Democrat, January 5, 1881; and Charleston News and Courier, May 11, 1881.

[26] Textile Record of America, April 1883, p. 105.

[27] Atlanta Constitution, January 6, 1881.

[28] Edward Atkinson to Nelson W. Aldrich, January 22, 1883, Atkinson Letterbook, Massachusetts Historical Society, Boston.

be entirely wiped off the tariff list. There is no greater difficulty in the way of Southern prosperity than this particular prohibition."[29]

The New Englanders prevailed, but the increase in the import tax on textile equipment further antagonized their upstart rival. *Dixie*, for example, bragged about the construction of new southern cotton mills "in spite of the enhanced cost of machinery caused by the legalized robbery known as the Protective tariff."[30] Many southerners rejoiced when the downturn in the business cycle in 1884 began to distress northern textile establishments. "A great many of them are now ready to shut down," the *Southern Industrial Review* reported with much delight.[31] "I still draw a grain of comfort from the present cotton goods depression," an important Augusta manufacturer crowed. "In this struggle caused by overproduction the fittest must survive." He shared the common assumption in his section that the New South would overpower New England in the fight for dominance in the textile business.[32]

The evidence does not support the traditional interpretation, most recently advanced by Paul M. Gaston in *The New South Creed*, which links the drive for southern industry with a desire for sectional amity. Actually, the reverse was true. It would appear that many historians have been misled by the fact that southern industrial promoters often tailored their arguments to fit the aspirations of their audience. While speeches prepared for home consumption usually bristled with anti-Yankee sentiment, propaganda designed to attract outside investment sometimes included rhetorical overtures calling for sectional reconciliation rather than economic retaliation. Henry Grady's frequently quoted address to the New England Society of New York in 1886 provides a classic example of the way militant southern industrial crusaders could mute their message. Gaston himself admits that "nearly every New South declaration of loyalty to the Union was also an appeal for Northern capital." He likewise suggests that southern spokesmen painted exaggerated pictures of economic success and racial harmony to stimulate northern investment in manufacturing in their region.[33]

---

[29] *Planters' Journal*, February 1883, pp. 30–31.

[30] *Dixie*, as quoted in *American Iron and Steel Association Bulletin*, January 6, 1886, p. 4.

[31] *Southern Industrial Review*, as quoted in *Boston Journal of Commerce*, May 3, 1884, p. 27.

[32] *Manufacturers' Record*, September 20, 1884, p. 167.

[33] Gaston, *New South Creed*, pp. 84, 95.

The depression between 1884 and 1886, however, frustrated the southern industrial drive. Cotton mill building declined sharply throughout the southern states. The number of charters issued to new cotton manufacturing corporations in South Carolina, for example, dropped from twenty-eight during the preceding boom years down to five during the economic slump.[34] Hours of operation were often reduced, and many small ventures failed. The larger and stronger establishments rode out the lean years by tightening their organizations, but even some of these firms experienced trouble. The profitable Graniteville Manufacturing Company, now under the able management of H. H. Hickman, lost money for the first time in more than seventeen years.[35]

But the upswing in the business cycle between 1887 and 1892 brought another burst in the construction of textile enterprises in the southern piedmont. Although there was some talk of furnishing these new undertakings with machinery capable of producing finer cloth, the bulk of the southern factories built during these flourishing years were equipped to manufacture coarse goods. The subsequent depression between 1893 and 1897 presented a serious challenge to the American textile industry, but optimistic southerners continued their mill building program in full stride. The number of cotton spindles in the four leading southern states increased by more than 200 percent during the 1890s, while the rate of growth in New England lagged far behind. Despite the hard times, southern factories were running more than a third as many spindles as their New England rivals by the turn of the century.[36]

Southerners owed much of their success in cotton manufacturing to their ample supply of cheap labor. Southern mill owners paid lower wages, ran longer hours, and employed more children than their northern competitors. While the number of operatives below the age of sixteen in New England factories declined from over 14 percent in 1880 to under 7 percent in the 1890s, the number in southern mills remained at about 25 percent throughout the period. The work week in the South averaged around sixty-six

[34] Gustavus G. Williamson, Jr., "Cotton Manufacturing in South Carolina, 1865–1892" (Ph.D. dissertation, Johns Hopkins University, 1954), Tables, n.p.

[35] Victor S. Clark, "Modern Manufacturing Development in the South, 1880–1905," in The South in the Building of the Nation, vol. 6 (Richmond, Va.: Southern Historical Society, 1909), p. 281.

[36] U.S., Department of Interior, Twelfth Census of the United States, 1900, Manufactures, 9, pt. 3: 46.

hours, compared to sixty in most northern states. Contemporaries repeatedly pointed out that low cost labor provided the cornerstone of the southern textile industry. Though estimates vary, historians generally agree that cheap labor gave the South its most important advantage over the North.[37]

Yet the spirit of the New South captivated the white operatives who formed the battalions in the cotton mill campaign. They showed respect and admiration for the textile directors who led their region in the struggle against Yankee domination. Despite the low wages and long hours, factory life represented a marked improvement over conditions prevailing in the countryside. Many mill hands, after fleeing from rural poverty and isolation, heard for the first time the sound of hard cash jingling in their pockets and experienced the new excitement of shopping for inexpensive consumer goods. Few ever returned to labor in the fields next to black neighbors. Those who felt mistreated by their employers frequently searched for a more benevolent boss in a nearby town. Most factory masters maintained a strong sense of social responsibility and governed their mill villages like antebellum plantations. They provided schools and churches, forbade drunkenness and prostitution, and kept a constant vigil over the material welfare and moral character of their people. Hence the paternalism that had emerged in the slave society of the Old South continued to discipline the free workers in the textile factories of the New South.[38]

Southern cotton manufacturers, however, were not above using harsh methods when their help broke the rules of the community by consorting with outside labor leaders. Wage cuts during the depression in the mid-1880s prepared the way for the Knights of Labor to organize southern textile operatives. In 1886 their efforts produced a great strike in Augusta which silenced most of the spindles in the city. The powerful Augusta textile executives

---

[37] Chen Chen-Han, "The Location of the Cotton Manufacturing Industry in the United States, 1880–1910" (Ph.D. dissertation, Harvard University, 1939), p. 410; Melvin T. Copeland, *The Cotton Manufacturing Industry in the United States* (Cambridge: Harvard University Press, 1912), pp. 36–43; Williamson, "Cotton Manufacturing in South Carolina," pp. 135, 159; and Melton A. McLaurin, *Paternalism and Protest: Southern Cotton Mill Workers and Organized Labor, 1875–1905* (Westport, Conn.: Greenwood Publishing, 1971), pp. 21–26.

[38] Cash, *The Mind of the South*, p. 205; McLaurin, *Paternalism and Protest*, pp. 38–39; and Dwight B. Billings, Jr., *Planters and the Making of a "New South"* (Chapel Hill: University of North Carolina Press, 1979), pp. 100–113.

quickly formed a business association and proceeded to stamp out the Knights. Besides suppressing union activity by discharging anyone connected with labor organizations, southern mill managers stifled local attempts to obtain legislation prohibiting child labor and reducing work hours in their plants.[39]

So armed with cheap labor, the captains of industry in the New South emerged triumphant in the first aim of the cotton mill campaign as they surpassed their New England adversaries in the production of coarse cloth. But they were unwilling to rest satisfied with that accomplishment. Blessed with the invention of the Northrop automatic loom, southerners advanced toward the second goal of their industrial crusade by capturing a share of the medium goods trade. The proportion of medium yarn spun in the South jumped from 3 to 26 percent of the nation's total output during the 1890s, and Massachusetts print manufacturers began to feel the effects of southern competition.[40] Yet the assault did not go uncontested. The corporations concentrated in the South Atlantic states encountered railroad freight rate discriminations when they purchased longer staple cotton from the Gulf states needed for making medium and finer fabrics.[41] Southerners were on the march, however, and in 1896 they proudly announced plans to erect a fine goods factory equipped to run on Sea Island and Egyptian cotton.[42]

As southerners commenced their invasion of the fields of finer production in the 1890s, they became interested in textile education. The *Charleston News and Courier* quickly began advocating the establishment of schools to provide the mechanical knowledge and skilled labor needed to enable the southern industrial soldier "to crowd all his competitors to the wall" in the medium and fine goods trade. Until such institutions were built, the editors complained, "we will have to content ourselves with making low-grade goods and leaving to the people of other countries, and of

---

[39] McLaurin, *Paternalism and Protest*, pp. 87–88, 105, 121–25.

[40] Blicksilver, *Cotton Manufacturing in the Southeast*, p. 21; and Thomas R. Smith, *The Cotton Industry of Fall River* (New York: King's Crown Press, 1944), pp. 80–121.

[41] *Transactions of the New England Cotton Manufacturers' Association*, April 28, 1897, pp. 92–93; *Boston Journal of Commerce*, May 7, 1898, p. 100; *Textile World*, September 1897, p. 29; and U.S., Congress, House, Industrial Commission on the Relations of Capital and Labor, Report, *House Document* No. 495, 56th Cong., 2nd sess., 1901, p. 491.

[42] *Manufacturers' Record*, June 26, 1896, p. 362.

other sections of this country, to pluck the richest fruits of our great staple crop."[43] Other southern papers joined the movement for technical education, and by the end of the decade state colleges in Georgia, the Carolinas, and Mississippi opened textile departments.[44]

Bitter memories of the Civil War and acute feelings of economic exploitation still stirred people in the defeated region as the nineteenth century drew to a close. Southern advocates of a new order continued to hope that the establishment of an extensive textile industry would stimulate general economic development in their part of the country. They remained confident that other manufacturing enterprises would follow the cotton factories to the cotton fields and that the subsequent urban growth would provide a local market for diversified agriculture. Southerners aspired to free themselves from the shackles of colonial bondage and to emerge victorious over their northern enemies in the fight for industrial supremacy. The vanquished people sought retaliation rather than reconciliation, and their cotton mill campaign involved a difference in tactics but not a change of heart. Thus the New South's struggle for economic independence marked a shift in the sectional conflict from the military arena to the industrial battlefield.

---

[43] *Charleston News and Courier,* as quoted in *Textile Record of America,* September 1890, p. 262.

[44] Copeland, *Cotton Manufacturing in the United States,* p. 138.

"Peace Hath Her Victories No Less Renowned Than War."

From *American Economist,* April 15, 1898.

Factories should be established in every part of the South, and instead of exporting cotton, export manufactured cotton goods.

Jackson Mississippian, 1866

The only criterion by which to determine the importance and prosperity of any country is the amount and value of its exports over and above its imports.

Governor Robert M. Patton of Alabama, 1866

We look forward to the time when all the cotton raised in the South shall be manufactured in the South. . . . The prospect before us in the South is a most inviting one, but we must have an outlet, we must have markets.

Senator Benjamin H. Hill of Georgia, 1879

We may go on building mills as hard as we please for the next fifty years, and we will not produce a greater effect on the cotton trade of the world than an additional river flowing into the ocean.

Charleston News and Courier, 1881

In the industrial readjustment that is taking place all over the world, only the fittest will survive, and Lancashire, which occupies an anomalous position in the world of the cotton industry, must be forced to the wall. . . . The legitimate successor to Lancashire is unquestionably the South.

Manufacturers' Record, 1892

Our foreign relations should be cultivated by way of anticipating our productive capacity. . . . We must have the people of the whole wide earth for our customers. It is commercial conquest upon which we should be bent. Unless the gates are forced open in some way, so that we may get to all markets on either hemisphere, we will be checked in our development.

John F. Hanson, Georgia Textile Manager, 1898

4

The New South's Quest for Commercial Empire

Southerners have traditionally regarded foreign commerce as vitally important to the wealth and welfare of their region. Economic life in the Old South revolved around the cultivation of a few primary crops produced mainly for long-distance trade, and by 1860 cotton alone made up better than half of the nation's total foreign sales. Although southerners devoted more attention to manufacturing in the postwar decades, they remained true to their export orientation. Spokesmen for the New South based their industrial crusade upon the assumption of a continually expanding overseas business. And their ambition to export manufactured articles in place of raw materials increasingly led them to try to influence the shaping of American foreign policy.

The New South program for economic development centered on a persistent drive to promote commercial expansion abroad rather than social regeneration at home. Conservative southern leaders quickly dismissed proposals for a radical redistribution of landholding designed to reduce rural poverty and to increase the local demand for industrial goods. They looked instead to foreign trade to stimulate cotton mill building and thereby create a home market for provisions. Southern commercial expansionists realized that the available labor supply was adroit enough to meet the needs of their export strategy. Southern workers lacked the skill necessary for spinning and weaving higher quality fabrics for domestic consumption, but they were quite capable of producing lower grade yarn and cloth suitable for the potentially vast markets in Latin America and Asia.

Southerners directed their cotton mill campaign toward foreign markets from the very outset. Newspapers throughout the defeated section in 1866 repeatedly linked their pleas for factory construction with their enthusiasm for commercial expansion. The *New Orleans Picayune* believed that the people in the cotton states should develop their textile industry to "the point of selling to the world the manufactured staple."[1] The *Jackson Mississippian* concurred. "Factories should be established in every part of the South," the editors urged, "and instead of exporting cotton, export manufactured cotton goods."[2] The *Montgomery Mail* likewise advised southerners to convert their raw fibers into rough fabrics before shipping them abroad in order to make their region "the seat of commercial empire."[3]

The expansionist consensus in the New South possessed influential and energetic leadership. Governor Robert M. Patton of Alabama, for example, again and again in 1866 called for the erection of cotton mills in the South. "We have, heretofore, been too much dependent upon the North for manufactured articles," he declared in typical fashion. Textile enterprises would not only allow southerners to become more self-sufficient, Patton argued, but they would also help them achieve a favorable balance of trade. "The only criterion by which to determine the importance and prosperity of any country," he reasoned, "is the amount and value of its exports over and above its imports." Patton was confident that his section could ship coarse cottons overseas and "compete successfully with Old England or New England or any other manufacturing country under the sun."[4]

Most southerners agreed. "We have every advantage," a Georgia industrialist explained in 1865, "plenty of water, cotton close at hand, and labor cheap."[5] If southerners would exploit these resources, the *Daily Columbus Enquirer* asserted in 1866, no other cotton manufacturing center "could then compete with us in the markets of the world."[6] The *Savannah Republican* expressed the prevailing sentiment a few years later. After the southern states

---

[1] *New Orleans Picayune*, as quoted in *Charleston Daily Courier*, October 17, 1866.

[2] *Jackson Mississippian*, as quoted in *Daily Columbus Enquirer*, June 27, 1866.

[3] *Montgomery Mail*, as quoted in *Daily Columbus Enquirer*, October 4, 1866.

[4] *De Bow's Review*, January 1867, pp. 56–68.

[5] U.S., Congress, House, *Executive Document* No. 34, 39th Cong., 1st sess., 1866. See Appendix to Special Report No. 3, p. 3.

[6] *Daily Columbus Enquirer*, May 19, 1866.

prepare themselves to fabricate their own cotton crop before sending it overseas, the editors boasted, they "will have no competition
in the markets of the world."[7]

Though the depression between 1873 and 1878 delayed cotton
mill building, southern leaders continued to entertain such visions
of imperial grandeur. Senator Lucius Q. C. Lamar of Mississippi
hoped that the Texas Pacific Railroad project would facilitate foreign trade and thereby help underwrite the drive for a new order
in his section. "The South has every condition of soil, climate, and
raw material for the development of a great industrial community," he noted. "But, to develop these industries, she must have
free access to the markets of the world." Desiring to reduce the
cost of transporting rough textiles to the Orient, Lamar advocated
the construction of "a railroad from the cotton fields of the South
to the Pacific."[8] Representative Hernando D. Money of Mississippi
even anticipated the acquisition of Hawaii as a stepping-stone to
the China market. "The march of empire is westward," he proclaimed, adding that "every people who have enjoyed Asiatic commerce have grown rich and prosperous."[9]

The depression experience reinforced the traditional export
commitment in the cotton states. As the domestic demand for textile products declined, southern mill owners sought relief in foreign markets. Some of the larger enterprises, like the Augusta
Manufacturing Company, remained able to pay handsome dividends during the lean years because they enjoyed a considerable
overseas business.[10] The lesson was not lost. Southern industrialists maintained their interest in foreign commerce when prosperity returned and factory construction resumed. Exports of
uncolored cloth jumped in value by more than three million dollars during the upswing in the business cycle between 1879 and
1883.[11] Although New England firms participated in this export
movement, a large proportion of the cotton goods shipped from

---

[7] *Savannah Republican*, as quoted in *De Bow's Review*, December 1869, p.
1075.

[8] U.S., Congress, Senate, *Congressional Record*, 45th Cong., 2nd sess., May 22,
1878, 7, pt. 4: 3653–59.

[9] U.S., Congress, House, *Congressional Record*, 44th Cong., 1st sess., April 6,
1876, 4, pt. 3: 2271–72.

[10] *Augusta Chronicle and Constitutionalist*, June 30, 1878.

[11] U.S., Department of Commerce and Labor, *Statistical Abstract of the United
States*, 1910, p. 491.

New York and Boston had been produced in the New South.[12] The model Piedmont Manufacturing Company was exporting more than half of its total output, and many newly established textile factories in Pelzer, Pacolet, and other nearby places in the South Carolina backcountry followed its lead.[13]

Southerners continued during these prosperous years to believe that their cotton mill campaign depended upon overseas economic expansion. "We look forward to the time when all the cotton raised in the South shall be manufactured in the South," Senator Benjamin H. Hill of Georgia explained in 1879. "The prospect before us in the South is a most inviting one," he continued, "but we must have an outlet, we must have markets."[14] Few disagreed. Until southern cotton factories add to their growing export trade, the *Manufacturers' Record* maintained in 1883, "we cannot hope to see this important branch of industry reach its proper development."[15]

Accordingly, southerners rapidly expanded their textile industry during the early 1880s in anticipation of a constantly increasing foreign commerce. The incorporators of new firms frequently announced their intention to produce coarse fabrics for export, while newspapers and business journals celebrating the cotton mill boom emphasized the great opportunity provided by overseas markets. "We may go on building mills as hard as we please for the next fifty years," the *Charleston News and Courier* assured its readers in 1881, "and we will not produce a greater effect on the cotton trade of the world than an additional river flowing into the ocean."[16] The *Manufacturers' Record* likewise assumed that foreign markets would be able to absorb the output of the rising cotton factories in the piedmont area. "Southern mills are beginning to compete quite strongly for the China trade," the editors crowed in 1883, "and we look for a still further growth of this business in the future."[17]

Southerners turned the widely publicized Atlanta Cotton Exposition held in 1881 into a conscious expression of their own

---

[12] *Charleston News and Courier,* August 1, 1881.

[13] *Manufacturers' Record,* February 1, 1883, p. 448.

[14] U.S., Congress, Senate, *Congressional Record,* 45th Cong., 3rd sess., February 20, 1879, 8, pt. 2: 1635–36.

[15] *Manufacturers' Record,* September 15, 1883, p. 139.

[16] *Charleston News and Courier,* April 12, 1881.

[17] *Manufacturers' Record,* May 3, 1883, p. 245.

expansionist dreams. They hoped that the affair would promote textile exports and thereby stimulate cotton factory construction in the southern states. Henry Grady's *Atlanta Constitution* predicted that the event would help open "the magnificent range of South American and Mexican markets."[18] Southern cotton manufacturers had already won the "first battle related to our home trade," the editor declared, and "there is no reason why the victory in the second and final contest need be less complete, especially in Mexico and all South American countries."[19]

The Atlanta Exposition featured a special consular report on "The Cotton Goods Trade of the World" and displayed it in the center of the Main Hall. Samples of textile fabrics used in various foreign countries accompanied the volume, which contained the views of commercial agents concerning market conditions in their respective districts. Senator John T. Morgan of Alabama had asked Secretary of State James G. Blaine to send these collections to Atlanta.[20] Blaine complied with the request and wrote back that the exhibit would be "a matter of great interest and profit to our cotton manufacturers and exporters."[21] Morgan was pleased. Later in the year, he called upon Congress to authorize the printing and distribution of several thousand copies of this instructive report showing that the market of the world furnished an "unlimited opportunity" for the cotton manufacturers he represented.[22]

The intimate relationship between the cotton mill campaign and the quest for commercial empire also manifested itself during the congressional debate in 1882 over immigration policy. California politicians, responding to the demands of labor unions, introduced bills to prohibit immigration from China. A few farsighted southerners expressed fear that an exclusionist law would seriously threaten their industrial development. They sympathized with the desire to check the number of Orientals coming into the country, but they wanted to achieve that objective without violating commercial treaties with China. These spokesmen for the New South did not want to alienate the Chinese government and

---

[18] *Atlanta Constitution*, December 4, 1880.

[19] *Atlanta Constitution*, February 25, 1882.

[20] U.S., Department of State, *Consular Report*, No. 12, June 1881, pp. 369–71.

[21] Blaine to Morgan, June 22, 1881, Record Group 59, Department of State, Domestic Letters, National Archives, Washington, D.C.

[22] U.S., Congress, Senate, *Congressional Record*, 47th Cong., special sess., October 15, 1881, 12, p. 524.

thereby jeopardize their growing sales of sheetings, shirtings, and drills in the Far East.

Senator Joseph E. Brown of Georgia took particular pains to explain why it was important for his section of the country to maintain friendly relations with the Chinese. "If we seek in the South to build up our infant manufacturing establishments," he argued, "there is no market in the world so inviting to us for the class of goods we make as the market of China." Since coarse cottons manufactured in the southern states were already meeting with great favor among the Chinese, he concluded that "it would be foolishness on our part to seek to wantonly offend these people, and destroy our influence and our commerce among them."[23] The *Atlanta Constitution* hailed Brown's speech as one of the most notable he had ever made on the floor of Congress. "There is much more in the Chinese problem than the shutting out of cheap labor from the Pacific coast," the editors pointed out. "The South is fast becoming a manufacturing section. The heavy goods usually made by southern mills are all best suited to China, and will surely find there a boundless market."[24]

Despite these commercial considerations, Congress passed an act suspending Chinese immigration for a period of ten years. Some southern political leaders registered opposition again in 1892 when Congress extended the exclusionist legislation. They agreed with Senator Morgan of Alabama that it would be "a very unwise step to put China into an attitude where she would break up her commercial relations with us."[25] Southern cotton manufacturers also warned that additional immigration restrictions might have disastrous consequences for their profitable Asian trade. These dire predictions ultimately proved correct when the Chinese retaliated by boycotting American goods soon after the turn of the century.[26]

Meanwhile, the slump in the business cycle between 1884 and 1886 presented a serious challenge to the New South's struggle for

---

[23] U.S., Congress, Senate, *Congressional Record*, 47th Cong., 1st sess., March 6, 1882, 13, pt. 2: 1639–40.

[24] *Atlanta Constitution*, March 10, 1882.

[25] U.S., Congress, Senate, *Congressional Record*, 52nd Cong., 1st sess., April 13, 1892, 23, pt. 4: 3563–65.

[26] *Asia, Journal of the American Asiatic Association*, February 8, 1902; and Howard K. Beale, *Theodore Roosevelt and the Rise of America to World Power* (New York: Macmillan, 1956), pp. 191–223.

industrial growth. Many small cotton factories closed, and plans for the construction of new establishments were put aside. Textile executives initially responded to the shrinking domestic demand with proposals for the formation of a pool to curtail production. The leading cotton mill owners in South Carolina and Georgia met in Augusta in 1884 to discuss schemes for limiting output, but they could not agree upon the proper method.[27] Another convention held in Augusta a year later failed to accomplish the same objective. This time most of the larger enterprises, which were heavily engaged in the export trade, did not even bother to send representatives to the meeting.[28] President C. J. Walker of the Charleston Manufacturing Company reasoned that foreign sales, "by taking so many goods out of the home market, will have all the effect of a shut-down, with less loss to the stockholders of the mills and without suffering to the operatives."[29]

Southern cotton manufacturers, in short, viewed expansion abroad rather than curtailment at home as the most promising remedy for their domestic ills. Hoping to increase their exports to Latin America, they succeeded in obtaining federal funds in 1884 to organize the New Orleans Cotton Exposition. Director General E. A. Burke explained that "the universal demand for new markets as an outlet for our surplus manufactures" had made the affair very popular among southerners. He shared their belief that it would create a "tidal wave" of trade with Spanish and Portuguese America.[30] Southern industrialists also looked to Africa to provide a vent for their accumulation of cotton goods during the depression. Always sensitive to the needs of the mill owners, Senator Morgan helped involve the American government in the Berlin Conference in 1884 in an effort to pry open the door to the Congo River basin.[31]

Southern textile leaders were convinced that their large shipments of coarse goods to Asia, Africa, and Latin America had helped them endure the depression. President Henry P. Hammett of the Piedmont Manufacturing Company in South Carolina wrote

---

[27] *Textile Record of America*, April 1884, pp. 108–9.

[28] *Boston Journal of Commerce*, July 4, 1885, p. 111; and August 8, 1885, p. 164.

[29] *Manufacturers' Record*, July 18, 1885, p. 711.

[30] *Boston Journal of Commerce*, May 31, 1884, p. 66.

[31] Tom E. Terrill, "The United States and the Congo, 1883–1885: The Second Liberia" (M.A. thesis, University of Wisconsin, 1963), pp. 60–61.

to one of his commission houses that foreign sales had saved many southern factories from shutting down during the hard times.[32] A New Orleans business publication made the same point. "The depression which set in during 1884," the *Cotton World* reported in 1887, "not only checked the organization of new mills, but crippled a good many institutions already in operation." Fortunately, the editors noted, the export trade had "afforded a relief from overproduction during the last two years."[33]

Southern cotton manufacturers sustained their commitment to overseas commerce during the economic revival between 1887 and 1892. Southerners constructed numerous factories equipped to manufacture rough textiles in these flourishing years, and they soon began to fear that domestic production would outstrip home consumption. "Southern cotton mills are pressing to the danger limit of overproduction of coarse goods," warned the *Manufacturers' Record* in 1889.[34] Concerned about the same problem, a southern industrialist maintained that a persistent effort to ship cotton fabrics abroad would be necessary in order to avoid "the old, old story—overproduction, the home market glutted, fall of prices, general stagnation, years of depression."[35]

Such apprehensions intensified the New South's export drive despite the upswing in the business cycle. Southern newspapers and periodicals often boasted during this prosperous period that a large number of textile enterprises in their section were sending a high percentage of their total output to foreign markets. Northern trade journals confirmed these reports. One Bostonian pointed out in 1888 that "Southern mills are now exporting more cotton fabrics to China than all New England."[36] As their heavy drills and sheetings began to displace English dry goods in northern China, the British consul-general at Shanghai lamented in 1892 that the Americans "are walking away from us."[37]

The New South's ability to compete successfully with Great Britain in the China market and elsewhere depended upon its cheap and tractable work force. Declining cotton prices caused many sharecroppers and tenants to flock to the factories as an

---

[32] Gustavus G. Williamson, Jr., "Cotton Manufacturing in South Carolina, 1865–1892" (Ph.D. dissertation, Johns Hopkins University, 1954), p. 103.

[33] *Cotton World*, September 17, 1887, p. 45.

[34] *Manufacturers' Record*, July 20, 1889, p. 11.

[35] *Boston Journal of Commerce*, February 25, 1888, p. 200.

[36] *Bradstreet's*, November 10, 1888, p. 719.

[37] *Bradstreet's*, September 10, 1892, p. 584.

escape from drudgery and disappointment on the farm. Technological advances in ring spindles allowed southern mill masters to tap this large supply of unskilled labor in their effort to dislodge England from its dominant position in the cotton goods trade of the world. "In the industrial readjustment that is taking place all over the world," the *Manufacturers' Record* declared in 1892, "only the fittest will survive, and Lancashire, which occupies an anomalous position in the world of the cotton industry, must be forced to the wall." The editors confidently concluded that "the legitimate successor to Lancashire is unquestionably the South."[38]

Southern leaders, prompted by this vision, urged the national government to cut a canal through Nicaragua to help them outmaneuver their British adversaries in the Far Eastern trade. Secretary H. G. Hester of the New Orleans Cotton Exchange was particularly fascinated by the prospect of having a cheap and speedy route to the Orient. "We need manufactures, but also a sure and lasting outlet for our manufactures," he exclaimed in 1892. "The cry is room; room for our manufactures!"[39] Many political spokesmen for the New South agreed that an interoceanic waterway would give southern cotton spinners a significant advantage in the potentially huge markets of Asia. Yet none fought harder than Senator Morgan of Alabama, who agitated the Nicaraguan question for twenty years. He believed that by exporting coarse cottons through the proposed canal the southern states could harvest the "wealth of the Indies."[40]

Southern expansionists also advocated various measures in an effort to outflank their British rivals in Latin America. While calling for reciprocal trade agreements in 1889, a prominent Augusta cotton mill owner explained that "what we want is a foreign market for our surplus goods."[41] Secretary of State James G. Blaine sympathized with their desire. Agricultural products would be the "best basis" for reciprocity with some countries, he wrote to President Benjamin Harrison, but "with others I think fabrics would be better."[42] Business journals praised Blaine in 1891 when he negotiated a treaty with Brazil providing for a 25 percent reduc-

---

[38] *Manufacturers' Record*, August 5, 1892, p. 10.

[39] U.S., Congress, Senate, *Congressional Record*, 52nd Cong., 2nd sess., January 14, 1893, 24, pt. 1: 561.

[40] Ibid., pp. 560–62.

[41] *Manufacturers' Record*, August 10, 1889, p. 15.

[42] Blaine to Harrison, July 24, 1890, Benjamin Harrison Papers, Library of Congress, Washington, D.C.

tion in duties on American cotton goods. President H. H. Hickman of the Southern Textile Manufacturers' Association was equally grateful. "Reciprocity," he predicted, "is the stepping-stone to an outlet for all our production."[43]

Southerners organized a combination of plaid manufacturers as a further technique designed to strengthen their competitive position in Latin American markets. The rapid expansion of the cotton plaid industry, particularly in North Carolina, led to the belief that production in this line had surpassed domestic requirements.[44] Most southern plaid makers, hoping to build up a profitable business in South America, agreed in 1891 to give the Cone Export and Commission Company exclusive control over their sales. Moses H. Cone explained that by carrying the accounts of several factories producing the same class of goods, his firm would be able to "stand the expense of looking up the foreign trade, which no single mill can do."[45] The Cone Company promptly dispatched an agent to Brazil, and it soon commenced making regular shipments of southern plaids to that country.[46]

Southern cotton manufacturers advocated federal appropriations for the merchant marine as still another tactic to help them win a larger share of the Latin American trade.[47] John F. Hanson of the Bibb Manufacturing Company of Georgia summarized their argument in a forceful address made in 1888 before the Southern Textile Manufacturers' Association. "The rapid growth of our cotton mills brings us face to face with a serious problem," he warned. Continued factory construction threatened to precipitate a crisis in the near future unless southerners drummed up "more consumers, new demand, new outlet." Latin American nations offered a vast market "for the excessive production of our mills at present, and for the output of those we are certain to build." But the South lacked sufficient means of communication with these countries. "In view of the situation that confronts us," he concluded, "there is no adequate remedy except in government subsidies to American shipping."[48]

---

[43] *Manufacturers' Record*, November 28, 1891, p. 8.

[44] *Boston Journal of Commerce*, August 10, 1889, p. 174.

[45] *Manufacturers' Review and Industrial Record*, June 15, 1891, p. 402.

[46] *Manufacturers' Record*, March 9, 1894, p. 9.

[47] See *Manufacturers' Record*, August 10, 1889, pp. 11 and 16, for responses to a questionnaire indicating that southern factory owners were generally strong advocates of government aid to the American shipping industry.

[48] *Manufacturers' Record*, December 8, 1888, pp. 11–12.

The members of the textile organization applauded Hanson's ideas and then by a unanimous vote appointed a committee to petition Congress for financial aid for steamship lines to ply between southern ports and South American markets. Hanson later sent a long letter to Secretary of State Blaine strongly urging subsidized shipping. "We cannot compete with England, France or Germany for this trade with Spanish America, while we are without prompt and regular mail and transportation facilities," Hanson argued. "If payment of the subsidies represents a contribution or so much loss by the government, as the representative of the people, and their aggregate interests, it is right that it should pay this loss from their common Treasury, and for their common benefit."[49]

Some southern politicians backed these demands for subsidizing the merchant marine. Representative George A. Tillman of South Carolina, for example, believed that his section needed improved connections with South America. Because the South required a "limitless market for its coarse cotton cloth," he reasoned, it had a "deep stake in opening up commerce with the countries below the Caribbean Sea." Tillman called upon his Democratic colleagues in the House to renounce any free trade doctrines that stood in the way of granting postal appropriations to the shipping industry.[50] Many southern congressmen and senators, however, repeated the standard argument that a downward revision of the tariff provided a better way to promote foreign commerce.[51]

Political leaders in the New South realized that the cotton manufacturers they represented had little need for protection because their coarse fabrics, like most southern agricultural commodities, were produced largely for overseas markets.[52] Politicians from North Carolina to Mississippi, moreover, generally subscribed to their section's traditional position that high tariffs threatened to undermine foreign trade. Even in Alabama, where

---

[49] Hanson to Blaine, July 20, 1889, Record Group 43, Records of U.S. Participation in International Conferences, Commissions, and Expositions, National Archives, Washington, D.C.

[50] U.S., Congress, House, *Congressional Record*, 49th Cong., 2nd sess., February 23, 1887, 18, pt. 3: 2158.

[51] See, for example, U.S., Congress, Senate, *Congressional Record*, 51st Cong., 1st sess., July 12, 1890, 21, pt. 8: 7180–81.

[52] See, for testimony showing that southern mill owners were generally uninterested in tariff protection, U.S. Congress, Senate, *Report* Nos. 469–474, 53rd Cong., 2nd sess., 1894.

some iron manufacturers advocated heavy duties, outstanding political figures like John T. Morgan, James L. Pugh, Hilary A. Herbert, and Joseph Wheeler refused to support a protectionist policy. And they felt vindicated during the depression of the 1890s when Alabama began exporting large amounts of pig iron as well as rough textiles.[53]

Southerners continued their cotton mill building program in full stride even as the business cycle spiraled downward between 1893 and 1897. They expanded the spindle capacity of old establishments and launched a great many new enterprises on the premise that a brisk foreign trade would compensate for the dragging domestic demand. Southern cotton manufacturers remained confident in their ability to vie successfully with Great Britain in the markets of the world. Daniel A. Tompkins, a leading textile spokesman in Charlotte, expressed the spirit of optimism that prevailed in his region. "England would be driven to the wall entirely," he boasted in 1893, "before the Southern mills would be reduced to the point of unprofitable operation."[54]

Southern industrial crusaders responded to the decline in home demand by increasing their efforts to penetrate foreign markets. They played a leading role in creating the influential National Association of Manufacturers as an institution designed to open export markets for cotton goods and other commodities. T. H. Martin, the editor of *Dixie*, offered the original idea in 1894. Explaining that domestic consumption could not keep pace with production, Martin urged that "an association of manufacturers be organized for the purpose of promoting trade with Mexico and South America."[55] Southern cotton mill owners welcomed his proposal. Soon after the NAM commenced operations, the Southern Textile Manufacturers' Association appointed a committee to cooperate with it "in matters pertaining to the extension of American trade."[56]

The NAM maintained a close watch over the expanding interests of the New South. President Theodore C. Search worked hard to enlarge the marketplace for yarn and cloth, and he received solid support from vice-presidents Ellison A. Smyth, John F. Hanson, and Daniel A. Tompkins—all prominent Southern textile ex-

---

[53] *Chattanooga Tradesman*, February 15, 1897, pp. 61, 78.
[54] *Manufacturers' Record*, April 14, 1893, p. 197.
[55] *Dixie*, October 1894, p. 30.
[56] *Boston Journal of Commerce*, May 30, 1896, p. 151.

ecutives. As factory construction continued in the South, *American Trade*, the official organ of the organization, revealed its concern about the glutted home market. "The capacity of American mills to spin and weave cotton is increasing more rapidly than the capacity of the people to wear the goods," the editors exclaimed in 1897. "The certainty that these conditions will continue compels the manufacturers to look abroad, not only to find present relief, but also to provide a future market."[57]

These apprehensions about domestic overproduction led southerners to intensify their agitation in behalf of an isthmian canal. The Dixieland press made strong appeals for the construction of an interoceanic waterway to reduce the cost of shipping rough cotton textiles to South American and Asian markets. Most southern politicians agreed that a canal should be built. "I do not think there is any difference of opinion among us as to the necessity of a canal across the isthmus," remarked Senator Benjamin R. Tillman of South Carolina.[58] Finally, in 1899, John T. Morgan succeeded in pushing a canal bill through the Senate. His constituency was happy. Morgan received many letters of congratulations, and the Alabama General Assembly adopted a joint resolution commending him for his tireless promotion of the project.[59]

Meanwhile, as the depression deepened in 1896, the New South once again toyed with the option of curtailing production. The Southern Textile Manufacturers' Association met in June of that year and passed a weak resolution calling for shutdowns arranged to "suit conditions governing different mills."[60] Yet it soon became apparent that only a few southern cotton manufacturers, other than the smaller ones producing colored goods, had any intention of reducing their output. Many larger firms, on account of their sizeable export trade, felt confident in their ability to run through the season without stopping.[61] The *New York Commercial and Financial Chronicle* summarized the situation in the South. "There

[57] *American Trade*, November 1, 1897, p. 16.

[58] U.S., Congress, Senate, *Congressional Record*, 55th Cong., 3rd sess., January 18, 1899, 32, pt. 1: 755.

[59] Bound Correspondence, Container No. 7, 1347–50, John T. Morgan Papers, Library of Congress, Washington, D.C.

[60] *Boston Journal of Commerce*, July 4, 1896, p. 228.

[61] *Boston Journal of Commerce*, July 18, 1896, pp. 260–61; July 25, 1896, p. 276; *Dixie*, August 1896, p. 32; *Manufacturers' Record*, July 17, 1896, p. 410; September 11, 1896, p. 108.

has been," it reported in September, "some resort to short time within the past month or two, but it has been sporadic rather than general. Southern mills have largely increased their export business, especially with China, to which country heavy shipments have lately been made, and at better prices than could be obtained for the same goods in the home market."[62]

The export trade did undoubtedly help protect many southern cotton manufacturers from the worst consequences of the depression. Informed sources clearly understood that the mills working on export goods were "the ones least affected by hard times."[63] President John H. Montgomery of the Pacolet Manufacturing Company reported in 1896 that his firm was being "considerably helped by orders for goods from China."[64] President H. H. Hickman of the Graniteville Manufacturing Company likewise pointed out that his concern was benefiting from an extensive foreign trade. "I have sold goods for China," he beamed, "for better prices than I can get from the home markets."[65] Reviewing the situation a year later, Moses H. Cone noted that the southern establishments which had large export contracts had done "much better than those which depended entirely upon our own home market."[66]

Since cotton mill owners had rejected the alternative of curtailing production during the depression, the political economy of the New South became more tightly tied to foreign commerce. Many leading southern textile enterprises were shipping a high proportion of their entire output overseas, particularly to the alluring China market. Between 1887 and 1897, while British exports of plain gray and white cottons to China decreased nearly 14 percent in quantity, American exports increased more than 120 percent.[67] Available statistics do not record the sectional origin of these shipments, but the evidence clearly indicates that the great bulk came from the South. To illustrate this point, a prominent New England industrialist pointed out in 1896 that "the marks on the productions of Pelzer, Piedmont and other southern mills are

[62] *New York Commercial and Financial Chronicle*, as quoted in *Manufacturers' Record*, September 18, 1896, p. 128.

[63] *Boston Journal of Commerce*, August 1, 1896, p. 293; see also *Bradstreet's*, June 27, 1896, p. 404.

[64] *Chattanooga Tradesman*, May 1, 1896, p. 104.

[65] *Manufacturers' Record*, July 31, 1896, p. 5.

[66] *Chattanooga Tradesman*, February 15, 1897, p. 87.

[67] U.S., Department of State, *Consular Report* No. 233 (April 1899), p. 560.

as well known among the Chinese as the 'Fruit of the Loom' or 'Lonsdale Cambrics' are here."[68]

Southern cotton manufacturers were convinced that their present prosperity and future welfare demanded a constantly expanding marketplace. On the negative side, they feared that a major decline in their export trade would force many already established factories to stop running their spindles and looms. On the positive side, they hoped that a growing overseas commerce would allow them to continue cotton mill building and thereby improve the general economic condition of their section. John F. Hanson of the Bibb Company articulated these emotions as the business cycle turned upward. "Our foreign relations should be cultivated by way of anticipating our productive capacity," he declared in 1898. "We must have the people of the whole wide earth for our customers. It is commercial conquest upon which we should be bent. Unless the gates are forced open in some way, so that we may get to all markets on either hemisphere, we will be checked in our development."[69]

Southern advocates of a new order had made an increasing effort to influence the conduct of American diplomacy during the last third of the nineteenth century. They believed that their drive to break the chains of a colonial economy at home depended upon commercial expansion abroad. Their desire to export rough fabrics rather than raw fibers led them to agitate for an isthmian canal, shipping subsidies, reciprocity treaties, and other measures calculated to strengthen their competitive position in foreign markets. Although the federal government did not grant all of their requests, southerners did begin to challenge Great Britain in the battle for supremacy in the cotton goods trade of the world. In other words, the New South's struggle for economic independence involved a continuing quest for commercial empire.

---

[68] *Manufacturers' Record*, June 5, 1896, p. 312.
[69] *Dixie*, February 1898, p. 26.

The man who will plant a full crop of cotton next year will, whatever he intends, prove an enemy to his section.

A Georgia Planter, 1867

If we were to take off one half of our cotton crop and devote our attention to the cultivation of grasses and the raising of live stock, as they do at the North, we could cut off one half of our expenses both in money and labor, and that money which we thus save we could put into a cotton factory and give us a market at home for all the products of our farm.

A Southern Granger, 1875

The State of Mississippi at present exempts cotton factories from taxation for ten years from the time they are built . . . but ten years are too little, let it be twenty years and it will be all the better.

President Frank C. Morehead,
National Cotton Planters' Association, 1881

The sooner we come to recognize the admirable adaptability of our State to a general system of diversified farming and industry, the sooner we will begin that steady growth and substantial progress which we all so much desire.

Progressive Farmer, 1887

We shall encourage more diversity of farming; the production of less cotton, more grain and meat; selling less raw material and more in manufactured articles.

A Declaration of Principles of the Southern Farmers' Alliance, 1887

It is the intention of the association to induce the farmer to build factories for manufacturing cotton near the cotton fields, so that the South may receive the largest returns from each annual cotton crop, and that home markets may be built up for all other farm products.

American Cotton Growers' Protective Association, 1897

5

Agricultural Businessmen in the New South

Standard accounts of the New South era remain under the spell of the progressive school of historiography. Writing in the shadow of Charles A. Beard, such eminent scholars as William B. Hesseltine and C. Vann Woodward depict the southern states during the postwar decades in terms of a fundamental conflict between town and country.[1] On the one hand, metropolitan businessmen and their political associates who looked forward to the growth of manufacturing are portrayed as colonial agents for northern economic penetration. On the other hand, farmers and planters are characterized as opponents of industrialism who wanted to return to the agrarian past. It is true that some antagonism between urban and rural interests did continue to stir southern politics in the postbellum period. Yet a closer examination of the movement to bring the cotton factories to the cotton fields indicates that studies picturing the New South as rent by a divided mind need serious revision.

The Civil War did not produce an internal revolution in southern society. As a result of the military ordeal, tenant farming and sharecropping replaced slavery, and some large estates changed hands. But most planters retained title to their land. The crop lien system, which allowed tenants to mortgage their staples to anyone

---

[1] C. Vann Woodward, *Origins of the New South, 1877–1913* (Baton Rouge: Louisiana State University Press, 1951); and William B. Hesseltine, *Confederate Leaders in the New South* (Baton Rouge: Louisiana State University Press, 1950). See, for a view contrary to the traditional interpretation, William J. Cooper, Jr., *The Conservative Regime: South Carolina, 1877–1890* (Baltimore: Johns Hopkins University Press, 1968).

advancing them supplies, did present a serious challenge to the planter class. Local merchants hoped to take advantage of the opportunity to extract most of the profit derived from southern agriculture by furnishing provisions, tools, and draft animals at high interest rates. But the planters increasingly appropriated the function of providing credit to their black tenants, thereby forcing the merchants to limit their lending operations to independent white farmers. Resting secure in their ownership of land and in their control of labor, the planters resumed their political hegemony over the South during the 1870s as Black Reconstruction came to a close.[2]

Like their associates among the planter elite, moreover, the Redeemer politicans who restored white rule in the southern states did not betray the economic interests of their section. The old Whigs and conservative Democrats who dominated the Solid South possessed similar attitudes toward industrial development.[3] Some politicians with distinguished records in the Confederate army did lend their names to Yankee firms, while other prominent officeholders served as supervisors in northern corporations operating in the South. Yet most who became involved in business affairs were not simply front men for outside interests. Many political leaders in the New South joined hands with metropolitan natives in sponsoring the cotton mill campaign. And, as the bulk of the money invested in textile factories came from within the region, these southern entrepreneurs reaped the benefits of ownership along with the rewards of management.[4]

These Redeemer politicans, moreover, were concerned about sectional prosperity as well as individual profits. The organization

---

[2] Jonathan M. Wiener, *Social Origins of the New South: Alabama, 1860–1885* (Baton Rouge: Louisiana State University Press, 1978), chaps. 1–4; and Dwight B. Billings, Jr., *Planters and the Making of a "New South"* (Chapel Hill: University of North Carolina Press, 1979), chap. 5.

[3] James T. Moore, "Redeemers Reconsidered: Change and Continuity in the Democratic South, 1870–1900," *Journal of Southern History* 44 (August 1978): 357–78. For a recent expression of the traditional view, see Paul M. Gaston, *The New South Creed: A Study in Southern Mythmaking* (Baton Rouge: Louisiana State University Press, 1970), p. 133.

[4] Broadus Mitchell, *The Rise of Cotton Mills in the South* (Baltimore: Johns Hopkins University Press, 1921), pp. 242–47, 267; Gustavus G. Williamson, Jr., *Textile Leaders of the South* (Columbia, S.C.: R. L. Bryan, 1963), pp. 507–8; and Holland Thompson, *From the Cotton Field to the Cotton Mill: A Study of the Industrial Transition in North Carolina* (New York: Macmillan, 1906), pp. 5–8, 81.

of the Southern Life Insurance Company illustrates their desire to augment the wealth and welfare of the entire region. President John B. Gordon and vice-presidents Benjamin H. Hill and Alfred H. Colquitt (all conservative Georgia Democrats) launched the enterprise in 1868 in Atlanta. The directors pointed out that before the war southerners had added to the economic strength of their enemies by allowing Yankee corporations to monopolize the insurance business. They called upon the former rebels to patronize southern insurance firms and thereby use their limited financial resources for their own enrichment.[5]

The Southern Life Insurance Company was initiated for the purpose of generating funds for the construction of cotton mills and other industrial establishments. "We already have a paying list of insured," Gordon wrote privately, "but I wish to do a much larger business and check more and more the drain of capital from our midst."[6] Soon after the venture had gotten off the ground, Gordon proudly reported to the stockholders that the institution was contributing to the "section's material independence."[7] The *Plantation*, speaking for agrarian interests in Georgia, praised the metropolitan undertaking in no uncertain language. "We wish," the editors exclaimed, "to see the drain of millions of dollars annually for life insurance from the suffering South to the plethoric North summarily stopped."[8]

Prominent planters likewise provided dynamic leadership in the New South's cotton mill campaign. Although a great many textile executives had urban backgrounds in banking and commerce, numerous others came from the ranks of the planter class. Dwight B. Billings, Jr., in *Planters and the Making of a "New South"* calculates that a majority of cotton mill owners in North Carolina were members of powerful landholding families. Declining cotton prices encouraged planters throughout the upper South to manufacture their crop, and the large white farm population in the surrounding countryside afforded a vast pool of cheap labor for the

---

[5] *Southern Recorder*, May 19, 1868.

[6] John B. Gordon to Benjamin C. Yancey, December 26, 1868, Yancey Papers, Southern Historical Collection, University of North Carolina Library, Chapel Hill. See, for similar motives behind the organization of the Mobile Life Insurance Company, H. M. Friend to Joseph Wheeler, October 27, 1874, Wheeler Papers, Alabama State Department of Archives and History, Montgomery.

[7] *Plantation*, June 25, 1870, p. 362.

[8] *Plantation*, July 29, 1871, p. 424.

rising textile establishments. But economic conditions in the deep South made agrarian leaders less inclined to risk funds in new business enterprises. Black belt planters enjoyed greater prosperity than their peers in the piedmont, and their region possessed a relatively small white yeomanry available for industrial work. Yet the evidence does not sustain the view of Jonathan M. Wiener in *Social Origins of the New South* that the power elite in Alabama opposed manufacturing. Even those Alabama planters who worried that iron factories would absorb their black field hands generally supported the cotton mill crusade which depended almost exclusively on white labor. Thus the decision to become a planter-industrialist rested more on material circumstances than on ideological predispositions.[9]

In every southern state, agricultural businessmen furnished solid support for the struggle to break the chains of a colonial economy. While many landless tenants and sharecroppers made specific complaints about such things as the credit crunch, most remained uninterested in the broader questions of sectional economic development. But the commercial farmers and planters (who made up the leadership and much of the membership for the state agricultural societies, the Grange, the Alliance, and finally the Populist Party) gave sustained backing to the drive for southern manufacturing. These politically influential agrarians likewise advocated a reduction in the number of acres devoted to cotton and an increase in the production of grains and meats.

The crop lien system, however, impeded agrarian reform in the cotton states. The merchants who supplied the small white farmers had first claim on their crops at harvest time. Narrowly preoccupied with their own self-interest, the tradesmen demanded that the yeomen plant more cotton for commercial exchange and grow less in the way of provisions for household consumption. In this way, the farmer would depend upon the storekeeper for his own food as well as for seed, fertilizer, and ginning services. The production of foodstuffs, by contrast, would give the merchant a less marketable yield and eventually destroy his credit business by releasing the farmer from the web of peonage. Excessive interest charges forced many of those in perpetual debt to sell their land to the very people who were exploiting them. The merchant who

---

[9] Billings, *Planters and the Making of a "New South,"* chaps. 4, 10; and Wiener, *Social Origins of the New South,* chaps. 5, 6.

became a landlord had even greater ability to compel his white tenants to raise cotton. As a result, the South was more tightly bound to a one crop economy.[10]

Agrarian spokesmen, nevertheless, began a long battle in the immediate postwar years against the temptation to return to the cultivation of cotton on a massive scale. They cautioned against succumbing to the lure of high prices and urged diversification in hopes of throwing off the shackles of the crop lien system. A Georgia planter expressed the prevailing sentiment when he declared in 1867 that "the man who will plant a full crop of cotton next year will, whatever he intends, *prove an enemy to his section.*"[11] An Alabama planters' convention a little later resolved that it had been a "grievous error" in the past to rely upon the Northwest for provisions, and it recommended a sharp curtailment in cotton production.[12] Despite such pleas, many decided once again to grow their traditional white staple. "They assume that little cotton will be planted by others," the *Southern Cultivator* regretfully explained in 1868, "that prices, therefore, will rule high, and if they raise large crops, their fortunes are secured."[13]

But a downward trend in cotton prices beginning in 1870 provoked widespread agrarian interest in textile manufacturing as well as diversified farming. The distressed tillers of the soil became increasingly attracted to the popular notion that the establishment of spinning and weaving factories would create nearby markets for a large variety of foodstuffs. Though few farmers had surplus funds, some planters did invest in industrial projects. Edmond Richardson, one of the largest cotton growers in the South, reorganized the Mississippi Manufacturing Company in 1873 after it had been destroyed by fire.[14] The success of his cotton mill at Wesson led to continued expansion through the reinvestment of profits, and Senator L. Q. C. Lamar of Mississippi happily noted that the enterprise had become "the subject of a great deal of pride and interest to the citizens of the state."[15]

---

[10] M. B. Hammond, *The Cotton Industry* (New York: Macmillan, 1897), pp. 142–51; and Wiener, *Social Origins of the New South,* p. 83.

[11] *Southern Recorder,* December 31, 1867. Emphasis in the original.

[12] *Southern Recorder,* January 7, 1868.

[13] *Southern Cultivator,* as quoted in *Southern Recorder,* March 10, 1868.

[14] *Planters' Journal,* January 1884, pp. 2–3; September 1884, pp. 70–71.

[15] L. Q. C. Lamar to Interstate Commerce Commission, May 11, 1887, Lamar Papers, Mississippi State Department of Archives and History, Jackson.

Meanwhile, the southern Grange, which reached its peak during the 1870s, persistently advocated the New South program of agricultural diversification and industrial expansion.[16] These two themes were nicely blended by C. W. Howard in "The Aims and Objects of the Patrons of Husbandry," a keynote address delivered in 1875 before an important Grange meeting in Charleston. The lecturer called upon the assembled farmers to lend a helping hand in constructing factories despite their own lack of cash. "If we were to take off one half of our cotton crop and devote our attention to the cultivation of grasses and the raising of live stock, as they do at the North," Howard proposed, "we would cut off one half of our expenses both in money and labor, and that money which we thus save we could put into a cotton factory and give us a market at home for all the products of our farm."[17]

The South Carolina State Grange avidly supported the industrial crusade. General Deputy D. Wyatt Aiken, one of the founders of the order, held the firm conviction that "the South needs cotton manufactures."[18] He constantly encouraged factory construction while serving as the editor of the *Rural Carolinian*, the semi-official organ of the organization. Aiken realized that the agricultural poverty accompanying the painful decline in cotton prices made it seem "like folly to talk of building up manufactures by the aid of farmers," but he refused to abandon hope that southern yeomen would unite at the county level and "contribute each a mite to erect a cotton manufactory at home."[19]

The South Carolina Agricultural and Mechanical Society also championed the New South's quest for economic independence and commercial empire. The principal paper presented to the organization in 1869 urged "the planters of the cotton-growing districts, all over the South, to combine together, in joint stock associations, and erect cotton mills." The appeal met with strong approval. A committee formed to promote manufacturing asserted that the production of "yarns and fabrics for export certainly ap-

[16] Theodore Saloutos, *Farmer Movements in the South, 1865–1933* (Berkeley: University of California Press, 1960), pp. 36–39; and J. H. Easterby, "The Granger Movement in South Carolina," *Proceedings of the South Carolina Historical Association* 1 (1931): 28–29.

[17] *State Agricultural Journal*, February 13, 1875, p. 3.

[18] *Rural Carolinian*, July 1873, p. 538.

[19] *Rural Carolinian*, September 1876, p. 402.

pears to be the policy and hope of the South."[20] A year later, William M. Lawton, a vice-president of the society, advocated the conversion of "raw cotton into yarns and diversified fabrics for export" in order to give the southern states "a destiny of unparalleled and boundless progress and prosperity."[21]

This mounting agrarian agitation for industrial development in South Carolina helped produce a favorable climate of opinion for the extension of public aid to private undertakings. The state's politicians responded promptly. The general assembly passed an act in 1873 excusing cotton mills and other new manufacturing projects from state, county, and municipal taxation for a ten-year period. Pleased with the measure, the *Rural Southerner* prodded the legislatures in other cotton states to "imitate the example of South Carolina" in stimulating the growth of infant industries.[22]

Agricultural periodicals published in Georgia likewise participated in the movement for an integrated economy based upon cotton manufacturing and mixed farming. The *Plantation* hailed the rise of southern textile factories in 1870 and hoped that they would provide the foundation for "commercial and financial independence."[23] In the same year, Georgia's farm journals applauded a widely reprinted essay suggesting that the state government grant tax exemptions to encourage the introduction of home industry.[24] Nor did this kind of propaganda go unheard. The Georgia General Assembly passed a law in 1872 giving a ten-year tax break to all money invested in new textile establishments. *The Southern Farm and Home* urged other cotton states to enact the same kind of "wise legislation."[25]

Agricultural spokesmen in North Carolina agreed that southerners should manufacture their own cotton before sending it to foreign markets. "In the new departure which the South has taken," the *Carolina Farmer* exclaimed in 1870, "the manufacturing interest is destined to wield a powerful and constantly increas-

---

[20] *Proceedings of the South Carolina Agricultural and Mechanical Society*, 1869, pp. 7–15.

[21] *Rural Carolinian*, January 1870, pp. 228–29.

[22] *Rural Southerner*, June 1874, p. 136.

[23] *Plantation*, April 30, 1870, pp. 232–33.

[24] *Southern Farm and Home*, January 1870, pp. 102–4; February 1870, pp. 132–35.

[25] *Southern Farm and Home*, November 1872, pp. 12–13.

ing influence in the realization of the imperial destiny which Providence has decreed for this section."[26] The editors hoped that their political representatives would speed the process in North Carolina by "exempting for five years all investments in manufacturing."[27] A member of the Grange proposed a longer period of governmental assistance. "Get the Legislature," he exhorted, "to exempt them from taxation for ten years."[28]

The official publication of the North Carolina Grange, the *State Agricultural Journal*, reflected the ardent rural support for the cotton mill campaign. "We have urged the importance of the establishment at home of suitable factories for the manufacture of cotton on several occasions," the editors admitted in 1874, "but we are persuaded that this great subject needs to be again and again pressed upon the attention of our people." The editors then advised farmers to use their "idle money that lies in drawers and chests, in old desks and stockings" for the construction of cotton factories which would provide a high return on their investments and create a home demand for their provisions. "Herein," the editors concluded, "the Patrons of Husbandry may do a great thing for North Carolina."[29]

Commercial farmers and planters in Alabama also backed the New South drive for economic diversification. The *Rural Alabamian* never tired of reprinting articles favoring the establishment of textile enterprises. Since agriculture and industry are "mutually dependent upon each other," the editors reasoned in 1873, "no State or country can be truly prosperous and great when either is neglected."[30] The editors believed that cotton mills would provide "the grandest and most efficient lever that will ever be used in lifting the Southern States out of their depressed condition." It was no exaggeration for the publishers to say that the subject of cotton manufacturing lay "nearest the editorial heart" of the paper.[31]

The leaders of the Alabama State Grange further revealed the strong agrarian commitment to textile manufacturing and improved farming. As the official mouthpiece of the organization, the

---

[26] *Carolina Farmer*, May 20, 1870, p. 6.

[27] *Carolina Farmer*, March 17, 1871, p. 4.

[28] *State Agricultural Journal*, July 31, 1875, p. 55.

[29] *State Agricultural Journal*, April 23, 1874, p. 2.

[30] *Rural Alabamian*, November 1873, pp. 490–91.

[31] *Rural Alabamian*, February 1873, p. 91.

Southern Plantation encouraged the Patrons of Husbandry in each county to invest in the construction of a local cotton factory.[32] William H. Chambers, the Worthy Master of the State Grange, joined the editorial staff in 1877. The paper soon changed its name to the *Farm Journal* because the publishers believed that the time had arrived for southerners to *"plant* less and *farm* more."[33] Almost simultaneously, Chambers helped establish the Alabama Industrial Association in an effort to promote the formation of an "industrial public opinion."[34]

Like their colleagues in other southern states, Grange leaders in Mississippi gave energetic support to the cotton mill campaign during the 1870s. E. G. Wall, the General Deputy of the State Grange, pushed hard for the construction of textile companies. He helped organize the order and then became the editor of its organ, the *Southern Field and Factory.* As the title suggests, this was a journal devoted to the New South program of agricultural diversification and industrial development. "We must encourage home manufactures and home markets," Wall counselled in a typical editorial, "and thereby keep as far as possible the profits of labor in our own State."[35] The paper frequently carried articles favoring mill building. "If Mississippi manufactured all the cotton produced within the State's confines," proclaimed one writer, "its wealth would be almost incalculable."[36] W. H. Worthington, the editor of the *Patrons of Husbandry,* made similar appeals to Mississippi Grangers to erect their own cotton factories.[37]

An air of confidence prevailed in the South, and numerous textile enterprises were projected throughout the region. The depression between 1873 and 1878, however, frustrated the movement for industrial expansion. The experience of the famous Piedmont Manufacturing Company under the skillful control of Henry P. Hammett in South Carolina dramatizes the difficulty encountered by those attempting to launch cotton factories. Hammett had been president of the Greenville and Columbia Railroad, and before the

[32] *Southern Plantation*, May 27, 1875, pp. 312, 315.
[33] *Farm Journal*, February 1878, p. 2. Emphasis in the original.
[34] Allen J. Going, *Bourbon Democracy in Alabama, 1874–1890* (Montgomery: University of Alabama Press, 1951), p. 115.
[35] *Southern Field and Factory*, April 1873, p. 187.
[36] *Southern Field and Factory*, March 1871, p. 120.
[37] James S. Ferguson, "Agrarianism in Mississippi, 1871–1900: A Study in Nonconformity" (Ph.D. dissertation, University of North Carolina, 1952), p. 225.

war he had helped his father-in-law run the Batesville Factory. Hammett organized the Piedmont Company in 1873, but the panic in that year delayed construction, and the firm did not begin actual operations for another three years. Many other promising efforts fared even worse, and shortages of capital resulted in the complete abandonment of several ventures.

Yet, even with these setbacks, the upturn in the business cycle in 1879 helped restore agrarian faith in the cotton mill campaign. That year a group of large and influential planters met in Vicksburg and founded the Mississippi Valley Cotton Planters' Association in order to promote multicrop farming and cotton manufacturing. President Frank C. Morehead set the tone at the opening convention by linking sectional economic development to overseas commercial expansion. Urging the planters to manufacture their great staple before shipping it abroad, Morehead predicted that the profitable business of exporting cotton fabrics would "reach into the billions."[38]

Though the organization changed its name in the following year to the National Cotton Planters' Association, the concern with improving southern economic life remained paramount. The *Planters' Journal*, the official organ of the association, was filled with articles suggesting different methods of reforming agriculture. The slogan on the title page—"Cotton and Grain Allies, Not Enemies"—underscored its persistent support for diversified farming. Convinced that the South could not thrive on a one crop basis, the editors urged the establishment of cotton factories to provide a home market for various products of the soil. They insisted that the demand created by mill towns would "double the profits now possible to the farmer in the majority of localities in the Cotton Belt."[39]

The Planters' Association aimed to "stimulate by any legitimate means home manufactures."[40] Under pressure from the agrarians, the Mississippi Legislature enacted a measure in 1881 sheltering new industries from taxation for ten years. President Morehead, still not completely satisfied, urged other cotton states to provide an even longer period of relief. "Ten years are too little,"

---

[38] *Augusta Chronicle and Constitutionalist*, July 22, 1879.
[39] *Planters' Journal*, August 1884, p. 34.
[40] *Planters' Journal*, January 1884, pp. 9–10.

he cried, "let it be twenty years and it will be all the better."[41] The *Planters' Journal* proudly listed the cotton mills already operating in Mississippi in 1882 and boasted that the new act would give rise to many more.[42] A year later, the association passed a resolution calling upon planters to "combine for the erection of cotton factories in our various communities."[43]

This powerful group of planters even put pressure on the national government to open Latin American markets for the output of their cotton mills. President Morehead succeeded in 1884 in getting federal funds appropriated for an exposition to be held in New Orleans.[44] The Board of Management, which included several key members of the Planters' Association, announced that the "leading object" of the exposition would be to gain new markets for manufactured goods. These southerners, having themselves experienced the hardships of a colonial economy, were quick to point out the advantages of trading the manufactured products of their section for the raw materials in underdeveloped Latin American countries. "Commercial exchanges with such countries are," the exposition managers asserted, "in accordance with sound laws of trade and political economy."[45]

Agricultural businessmen who operated on a small scale likewise remained committed to the creed of the New South. Commercial farmers in Mississippi, for example, maintained their agitation in behalf of a balanced economy. Eagerly anticipating the time when the southern states would become a great cotton manufacturing center, the *Rural Mississippian* believed in 1882 that "the profits of planting, which used to be invested in slaves, will be invested in spindles."[46] The Patrons of Husbandry in Mississippi continued to hope that factory construction would increase the local demand for farm produce. "With food crops making us a self-sustaining people, and cotton as a surplus," the Holmes County Grange proclaimed in 1884, "we can at no distant

---

[41] *Textile Record of America*, June 1881, p. 136.

[42] *Planters' Journal*, November 1882, p. 128.

[43] *Planters' Journal*, January 1884, p. 34.

[44] U.S., Congress, Senate, *Executive Document* No. 18, 49th Cong., 1st sess., 1885, pp. 11–12.

[45] U.S., Congress, Senate, *Congressional Record*, 49th Cong., 1st sess., June 28, 1886, 17, pt. 6: 6201–03.

[46] *Rural Mississippian*, February 1882, p. 9.

day be as prosperous as any people living on the habitable globe."[47]

Nonetheless, these rosy dreams could not avert the wave of farm protest which spread across the southern states during the 1880s. The agrarian discontent had several sources. Declining cotton prices pinched large planters and independent farmers while the crop lien system continued to burden smaller operators in particular. The protective tariff, expensive fertilizer, and high railroad freight rates provided added grievances that sparked the Farmers' Alliance movement in the South.[48] The Southern Alliance leaders focused their attention on establishing producer and consumer cooperatives designed to make members less dependent upon local merchants. These cotton exchanges promised to help farmers sell their crops at optimum prices and to obtain their supplies cheaper through wholesale buying.[49] Though increasingly bitter about the shortage of money, few Alliancemen ever opposed free enterprise. Most conceived of themselves as agricultural businessmen who were combining to protect their economic interests, and many believed that the rise of industry would enhance the welfare of agriculture.

Southern Alliance leaders often denounced "monopolists" for their greedy practices, but at the same time they commended "honest" industrialists engaged in developing the region. Prominent cotton manufacturers like Thomas M. Holt of North Carolina and John F. Hanson of Georgia were on occasion singled out for special praise.[50] The *Southern Alliance Farmer* pointed out why the agrarians harbored little hostility for mill owners. "It is a fact that the spinner is not the man who corners our crop or forces its price below its cost of production," the editors explained, "but the speculator who buys up the crop and sells to the spinner as his trade demands it and makes a good profit by the transaction."[51]

The Southern Farmers' Alliance, like the Grange before it, was bound to the ideology of the New South. A declaration of princi-

---

[47] *Minutes of the Holmes County Grange*, April 10, 1884, Mississippi State Grange Papers, Mississippi State Department of Archives and History, Jackson.

[48] Woodward, *Origins of the New South*, pp. 180–86.

[49] Robert C. McMath, Jr., *Populist Vanguard* (Chapel Hill: University of North Carolina Press, 1975), pp. 53–54; and Lawrence Goodwyn, *Democratic Promise* (New York: Oxford University Press, 1976), p. 196.

[50] *Progressive Farmer*, November 17, 1886, p. 4.

[51] *Southern Alliance Farmer*, October 14, 1890, p. 4.

ples made by the Southern Alliance in 1887 revealed the basic orientation: "We shall encourage more diversity of farming; the production of less cotton, more grain and meat; selling less raw material and more in manufactured articles."[52] A year later, an Alliance meeting in Raleigh similarly illustrated the trend in thinking in this resolution: "WHEREAS, diversified agriculture is the true theory for successful farming, and whereas, diversified agriculture is dependent on diversified manufacturing for its development, *Resolved*, That it should be the policy of the southern farmer to encourage manufacturing enterprise."[53]

Deeply troubled by dropping cotton prices, agrarian protestors repeatedly urged crop diversification. An interstate agricultural convention held in Atlanta in 1887 proclaimed that "the true policy of the southern farmer is to make his farm self-sustaining and make his cotton his surplus."[54] Another group of cotton growers, including many Alliancemen, met in Atlanta and offered the same argument a few years later.[55] Southern political leaders had already taken the cue. Senators Matthew C. Butler of South Carolina, James Z. George of Mississippi, and John T. Morgan of Alabama played an active part in the effort in 1887 to get federal appropriations for the establishment of state agricultural experimental stations. They hoped that the research centers funded by the Hatch Act would facilitate the use of improved farming techniques in their section.[56]

Southern Alliance organs, in line with the resolutions and declarations put forth at numerous conventions, advocated a reduction in cotton production. The *National Economist*, under the editorship of C. W. Macune, stood almost alone in opposition. "It is a mistake to urge people of the cotton belt to raise less cotton and more corn," the editor insisted in 1890. "Instead of undertaking to diversify industries, let the people of that section devise means whereby a fair price can be obtained for what they now produce."[57] Acting on his own advice, Macune advanced the sub-

---

[52] *Progressive Farmer*, November 10, 1887, p. 4.

[53] *Progressive Farmer*, September 4, 1888, p. 1.

[54] *Progressive Farmer*, September 22, 1887, p. 2.

[55] *National Economist*, Nobember 14, 1891, p. 136; and *Transactions of the South Carolina Agricultural and Mechanical Society*, 1891, p. 78.

[56] U.S., Congress, Senate, *Congressional Record*, 49th Cong., 2nd sess., 18, pt. 1: 720–30; and pt. 2: 1038–45, 1077–82.

[57] *National Economist*, January 25, 1890, pp. 296–97.

treasury plan to counter the maneuvers of speculators who bought up the whole cotton crop at low prices in the fall when the market was glutted. The proposal called for creating federally financed warehouses and extending short-term credit to farmers to allow them to hold back part of their crop in order to keep prices stable throughout the year.[58]

Macune's plan provoked harsh criticism. It was not at all surprising that opponents offered the New South strategy as the only viable alternative to the suffering farmers. Congressman Joseph Wheeler of Alabama maintained that the establishment of a subtreasury would be "a step in the wrong direction." He advocated the exact "opposite plan" of cotton manufacturing. "The immensely increased population required for this work," Wheeler asserted, "would cause a demand for all the breadstuffs, meats, and vegetables we could raise in the South."[59] Senator George of Mississippi also came out forcefully against the subtreasury idea and argued that manufacturing would provide the only effective means of keeping money in the state.[60]

Yet Macune had been the president of the Southern Farmers' Alliance, and his grandiose scheme attracted a wide following. While many urban business interests quickly registered their objection, some notable industrialists expressed considerable sympathy for the troubles of agrarians in their section. John F. Hanson of the Bibb Manufacturing Company in Macon, for example, wrote in favor of the subtreasury plan.[61] Angry farmers were much more enthusiastic in their support. But while Southern Alliance members generally backed Macune's proposal, they did not share his disregard for diversified agriculture. Few ever gave up their struggle for an integrated economy, and in some counties Alliancemen pooled their resources and succeeded in building local cotton factories.[62]

Leonidas L. Polk, much more than Macune, represented the

---

[58] *National Economist*, September 21, 1889, p. 9.

[59] U.S., Congress, House, *Congressional Record*, 51st Cong., 1st sess., August 1, 1890, 21, Appendix: 672–78.

[60] James Z. George Scrapbook, Mississippi State Department of Archives and History, Jackson.

[61] *Southern Alliance Farmer*, October 14, 1890; and *Dixie*, September 1899, p. 23.

[62] *Progressive Farmer*, February 5, 1889, p. 1; and William W. Rogers, "The Farmers' Alliance in Alabama," *Alabama Review* 15 (January 1962): 13.

dominant outlook of the Southern Alliance. The former Confederate army officer was deeply touched by the economic plight of his section. While active in setting up the North Carolina Grange in the 1870s, Polk began preaching the doctrine of multicrop farming. He also worked closely with Thomas M. Holt in advocating tax exemptions for new cotton mills.[63] As cotton and tobacco prices dropped lower and lower during the 1880s, Polk once again helped organize southern farmers to enhance their position in the marketplace and to improve the financial condition of the entire region. Polk maintained his strong commitment to the New South program when he became the president of the Southern Alliance at the end of the decade.

Polk founded the *Progressive Farmer* in 1886, and the paper soon became the official organ of the North Carolina Alliance. From the outset, Polk's editorials persistently stressed the popular themes of cotton mill building and agricultural reform. "The sooner we come to recognize the admirable adaptability of our State to a general system of diversified farming and industry," a characteristic editorial remarked, "the sooner we will begin that steady growth and substantial progress which we all so much desire."[64] Polk, like so many other agricultural businessmen in the South, defined progress in the same terms as his metropolitan friends. In the early 1890s, for example, he frequently ran a front-page column listing new southern industries reprinted from the *Manufacturers' Record* under the title of "Our Progress."

Polk's career dramatizes the conservative nature of the leaders that inspired the Populist revolt in the South. After the failure of the Alliance exchanges, southern farmers concluded that they would have to win political power in order to influence national monetary policy. Wishing to repay their debts in debased currency, many entered the People's Party, which demanded the unlimited coinage of silver to increase the quantity of money in circulation. Populist leaders, like Polk, were substantial property owners who hoped to reform the capitalist system in the interest of commercial agriculture.[65] They did not want to articulate the basic antagonism between landlords and tenants. Polk used his position in the white Alliance in 1891 to defeat a proposal made by the Colored

---

[63] Stuart Noblin, *Leonidas LaFayett Polk, Agrarian Crusader* (Chapel Hill: University of North Carolina Press, 1949), pp. 95–101, 134–40.

[64] *Progressive Farmer,* April 21, 1887, p. 2.

[65] Billings, *Planters and the Making of a "New South,"* p. 183.

Alliance urging black cotton pickers to strike for higher wages.[66] Polk died before he could become the presidential candidate for the People's Party in 1892, but his Populist colleagues continued to be more interested in changing the relationship between different sections than among social classes.

Agricultural businessmen in the New South carried on the industrial campaign during the last decade of the century. In response to continually declining prices for their staple crop, planters from several southern states gathered in the winter of 1894–95 to organize the American Cotton Growers' Protective Association. The opening convention passed resolutions calling for a cutback in cotton acreage and an increase in the production of cereals and the raising of livestock. The planters also urged the stimulation of industry by "exempting manufactories from taxation for a period of ten years."[67] A few years later, the association announced its intention to "induce farmers to build factories for manufacturing cotton near the cotton fields, so that the South may receive the largest returns from each annual cotton crop, and that home markets may be built up for all other farm products."[68]

Meanwhile, southern factory owners were soliciting agrarian aid in opening foreign markets for cotton goods. President H. H. Hickman of the Southern Manufacturers' Association called upon Alliancemen in 1891 to "help us in our efforts to open up our trade to other countries, and after a while we can buy all your cotton and pay you better prices for it."[69] President Daniel A. Tompkins of the Southern Cotton Spinners' Association agreed that the interests of "the Southern manufacturer and the Southern cotton farmer all lie together in the development and maintenance of our export trade." Tompkins explained that overseas markets for cotton goods would spur factory construction and thereby raise the price of cotton and "also create home markets for other farm products."[70]

---

[66] Robert L. Allen, *Reluctant Reformers: Racism and Social Reform Movements in the United States* (Washington, D.C.: Howard University Press, 1974), p. 61.

[67] *Chattanooga Tradesman*, December 1, 1894, pp. 84–85. See also February 1, 1895, p. 67.

[68] *Chattanooga Tradesman*, January 1, 1898, p. 128. See also *Bradstreet's*, December 25, 1897, p. 822.

[69] *Manufacturers' Record*, November 28, 1891, p. 8.

[70] Daniel A. Tompkins, *American Commerce, Its Expansion: A Collection of Addresses and Pamphlets Relating to the Extension of Foreign Markets for American Manufacturers* (Charlotte, N.C.: published by the author, 1900), pp. 91–94.

Farm protest leaders in North Carolina, like their counterparts elsewhere in the South, accepted the basic program for economic development advanced by the metropolitans. Populist Representative Harry Skinner hoped southerners would manufacture all the cotton produced in their region. "We would simply convert a three-hundred-million dollar crop into a nine-hundred-million dollar crop," he calculated, "and build up a home market for diversified products."[71] Marion Butler, soon to become a Populist senator, similarly linked agricultural prosperity to industrial growth. He urged southerners to export rough textiles rather than raw cotton and thereby follow the same road that led both Old England and New England to wealth and power.[72]

The bond cementing town and country interests in the southern states did not dissolve at the water's edge. Overseas commercial expansion promised to stimulate continued cotton mill building, and the rise of urban centers in turn would open the way for agricultural reform. The whole strategy depended upon cheap factory labor which enabled the industrialists to compete successfully in the markets of the world. The agrarians had no more quarrel with the exploitation of the mill hands than with the exportation of the textile products. Child labor and long hours in the factories gave southern farmers little cause for complaint since they often worked themselves and their own children in the fields from dawn until dusk. Thus, farm protest leaders like Benjamin R. Tillman of South Carolina spurned northern proposals for legislation to reduce hours of labor in southern industry. "I do not think," Tillman gloated, "the country is going to get up any protective tariff within this Union for the benefit of New England."[73]

This consensus uniting city and farm provided the foundation for the cotton mill campaign which so excited Dixieland during the last three decades of the nineteenth century. Rural leaders joined with their urban neighbors in directing the southern crusade against northern domination of their economy. The commercial farmers and planters, who remained a strong political force in the southern states, supported their industrial friends with deeds

---

[71] U.S., Congress, House, *Congressional Record*, 55th Cong., 1st sess., March 25, 1897, 30, pt. 1: 308–12.

[72] Marion Butler, "The Hour's Need," February 12, 1886, Butler Papers, Southern Historical Collection, University of North Carolina Library, Chapel Hill.

[73] U.S., Congress, Senate, *Congressional Record*, 55th Cong., 2nd sess., 1898, 31, pt. 2: 1033.

as well as words. These agrarians not only voted in favor of tax exemptions for new manufacturing enterprises, but many also invested their own savings in local textile factories. The New South's quest for economic independence and commercial empire, then, was based upon a solid alliance between metropolitan and agricultural businessmen.

From Daniel A. Tompkins. *Cotton Mill, Commercial Features.* 1899.

I have been compelled to change my views very materially of the chance of the Southern manufacturer being rather more of a competitor than we are anxious to have.

Report to the New England Cotton Manufacturers' Association, 1881

The chief obstacle to the extension of southern cotton manufacturing now consists in the heavy duties on iron and steel, the effect of which is to make the cost of cotton machinery about one third greater than it is in Europe.

Edward Atkinson, Boston Industrialist, 1883

They are fast on the heels of the north, and the only way we at the north can lead the procession and run our mills at a profit is to get onto finer goods.

Boston Journal of Commerce, 1891

The competition affects all kinds of goods manufactured in New England, because if too many coarse goods are manufactured the mills here will be driven to fine goods, and then too many fine goods will be made.

T. Jefferson Coolidge, Boston Textile Executive, 1896

The cotton mills are suffering from Southern competition, which by child labor, long hours, and low wages, put us at a disadvantage. . . . The Southern operatives must be brought up to our standard. . . . To this important work I hope our labor unions will address themselves.

Senator Henry Cabot Lodge of Massachusetts, 1898

It is agreed on all sides that the National Congress should fix the hours of labor and in general control labor legislation, so that there may be uniformity in all the States.

Report of the Committee on Labor in the Massachusetts Senate, 1898

6

New England's Reaction to the New South

Spokesmen for the New South frequently complained that Yankee businessmen and politicians were doing everything in their power to hinder southern industrial development. Northern leaders not only denied these accusations, but many went further to assert that they welcomed southern efforts to become more like themselves. Such claims and counterclaims raise an intriguing historical problem: did the private attitudes of northerners correspond with their public pronouncements? This question is especially interesting when applied to the New England cotton manufacturers who, more than any other northern business group, met stiff competition from the southern states during the last two decades of the nineteenth century.

In the antebellum period, southern industrial promoters had launched a cotton mill campaign to spearhead their struggle to obtain relief from the ills of a one crop economy. These advocates of a New South assumed that the establishment of textile enterprises would open the way for the introduction of related industries. They believed that the growth of urban centers in turn would increase the local demand for farm produce and make their region less dependent upon cotton culture. The clamor for economic diversification varied with the market value of the South's great agricultural staple. Depressed cotton prices in the 1840s provoked heightened agitation for home manufacturing, and during the latter part of the decade the southern states enjoyed a spurt in the construction of small factories outfitted to transform their raw fibers into rough fabrics.

The New England coarse cloth manufacturers, in the mean-

time, were experiencing difficulty caused by a drop in overseas
demand for their products. The larger Massachusetts textile establishments, owned by Boston capitalists like Amos A. Lawrence,
suffered particularly from a decline in their China trade. The rising
cotton mills in the South threatened to give the New Englanders
additional trouble. In November 1849 General Charles T. James
made matters worse by writing a widely publicized article for
Hunt's Merchants' Magazine calling attention to northern industrial profits and advertising southern advantages for cotton manufacturing. James, a Rhode Island machine maker, hoped to build
up a southern market for textile equipment, but his gains would
come at the expense of the Massachusetts factory masters.

Amos A. Lawrence almost immediately began preparing an argument to deny the notion that northern textile corporations were
paying handsome dividends and to deter southerners from erecting more spinning and weaving enterprises. Lawrence privately
expressed the fear that the piece by James would "add to the excitement which now exists in favor of manufacturing at the
South."[1] While organizing his brief, he requested data from the
Naumkeag Mills to bolster his case designed to "check the over
growth of factories which already presses us down."[2] A representative of the company responded by suggesting that James might
be bribed to keep quiet since he could "not be making a great deal
of money."[3] But James was not to be silenced, and Lawrence soon
published a rebuttal in *Hunt's*. His uncle later congratulated him
on his attempt to discourage industrial development in the cotton
states. "Our Southern friends," he noted wryly, "will read and
ponder."[4]

William Gregg, the leading South Carolina cotton manufacturer, tried to protect his section from the conflicting interests
underlying the controversy between the Rhode Island machine
builder and the Massachusetts mill owner. "The low dividends of
Mr. Lawrence, and the high estimate of profits of General James,
are both calculated to mislead," Gregg charged in an essay in

---

[1] Amos A. Lawrence to N. Silsbee, Jr., November 19, 1849, Lawrence Letterbook, Massachusetts Historical Society, Boston.

[2] Ibid.

[3] N. Silsbee, Jr., to Amos A. Lawrence, November 21, 1849, Lawrence Correspondence, Massachusetts Historical Society, Boston.

[4] Abbot Lawrence to Amos A. Lawrence, February 25, 1850, Lawrence
Correspondence.

Hunt's. The large subscriptions of stock in the New England cotton factories, he reasoned, made it obvious that Yankee entrepreneurs were receiving at least modest returns on their investments. Gregg pointed out, furthermore, that both antagonists had neglected to make the crucial distinction between individual earnings and regional prosperity. "Eastern people," he asserted, "have grown rich from a pursuit which has paid capitalists only a moderate interest on their money." He concluded that southerners should follow the same road to wealth and power.[5]

Failing to dampen southern enthusiasm for cotton manufacturing, some New England business leaders next began thinking in terms of turning to the production of finer cloth to escape competition from the South. Lawrence warned his uncle in 1850 that southerners would continue to expand their capacity for making coarse cottons, and he suggested that an increase in tariff rates on finer goods would allow northerners to make more expensive merchandise.[6] Lawrence emphasized the same point in a letter to Senator Robert C. Winthrop of Massachusetts. "A higher Tariff, or rather a change from ad valorem to specific duties," he advised, "would enable us to advance in manufacturing, by creating new fabrics, whereas now we must *stand still.*"[7]

Northern apprehensions about southern industrial rivalry waned in the 1850s as increased cotton prices made planters less inclined to risk funds in unfamiliar business ventures. While capital continued to flow into agriculture, the southern textile industry remained small. Then the Civil War reduced the rebel states to an impoverished condition. Despite severe money shortages during the reconstruction era, southerners revived their antebellum dreams for a balanced economy. Numerous textile establishments were projected throughout the South, but the harsh depression between 1873 and 1878 frustrated the movement to bring the cotton factories to the cotton fields. Hence the lords of the loom in New England rested secure in their industrial supremacy.

But the return to prosperity between 1879 and 1883 sparked a dramatic cotton mill boom in the piedmont area of the South Atlantic states. The sudden surge in southern spindle capacity sent

---

[5] *Hunt's Merchants' Magazine,* January 1850, pp. 107–8.

[6] Amos A. Lawrence to Abbot Lawrence, December 19, 1850, Lawrence Letterbook.

[7] Amos A. Lawrence to Senator Robert C. Winthrop, August 20, 1850, Lawrence Letterbook. Emphasis in the original.

a wave of anxiety through northern business circles. "We felt no danger from the South until 1880," explained T. Jefferson Coolidge, a prominent New England textile executive. "Then the cloud was no bigger than a man's hand, but it was there and was threatening us."[8] *Bradstreet's* warned in 1880 that "it would not be surprising if the centers of cotton manufacture gradually drifted in a southerly direction."[9] A few years later, the *Boston Commercial Bulletin* complained that South Carolina and Georgia mills were competing with Massachusetts factories in foreign as well as domestic markets. The editors worried that before long the cotton states would "practically monopolize the manufacture of the coarser and heavier grades of goods."[10]

The Atlanta Cotton Exposition held in 1881 brought the sectional economic conflict to the fore. The initial impetus came from the North. The members of the New England Cotton Manufacturers' Association had been especially concerned about the poor quality and bad condition of the raw material they were receiving from the South.[11] Edward Atkinson, representing the northern business group, suggested the organization of an exposition devoted to improving the cultivation and handling of the cotton crop. Southerners backed the proposal for their own purposes and insisted that the event be held in Dixie. They hoped the exposition would help propel their region into a new era by stimulating investments in textile manufacturing. Northern machine makers, desiring to increase their southern sales, likewise supported the project.[12]

Like Lawrence in his earlier efforts, however, Atkinson tried to steer southern industrial boosters away from their commitment to economic diversification. He advised southerners to concentrate their energy on "ginning, packing, and preparing cotton for the use of the factories" and to leave the manufacturing end of the operation to northerners. Atkinson visualized the future development of

---

[8] *Chattanooga Tradesman*, April 15, 1895, p. 83.

[9] *Bradstreet's*, March 10, 1880, p. 4.

[10] *Boston Commercial Bulletin*, as quoted in *Manufacturers' Record*, April 5, 1883, p. 149.

[11] Harold F. Williamson, *Edward Atkinson: The Biography of an American Liberal, 1827–1905* (Cambridge, Mass.: Riverside Press, 1934), pp. 166–67.

[12] Jack Blicksilver, "The International Cotton Exposition of 1881 and Its Impact upon the Economic Development of Georgia," *Cotton History Review* 1 (October 1960): 176–78.

the South along lines which would be supplementary and not antagonistic to northern economic interests.[13] But southerners reacted bitterly to his idea that they should remain on the agricultural half of an imperial relationship with the industrial North. They denounced Atkinson and boasted that their region would become the seat of cotton manufacturing in the country. Their resentment took concrete form when the very exposition building which Atkinson had suggested might be removed in pieces and utilized for ginning cotton was instead converted into an impressive textile factory.

The Atlanta Exposition received widespread publicity and made northerners even more conscious of the New South's determination to free itself from the fetters of a colonial economy. *Bradstreet's* announced that the affair demonstrated that southerners intended to fabricate their own crop. "They are not content to remain the growers of four-fifths of the cotton of the world. They propose to make the attempt to share the profits that come from the manufacture of cotton goods." The journal warned northern mill owners that they would face "a difficult competition to overcome."[14] Richard Garsed, an official representative of the New England Cotton Manufacturers' Association, was equally alarmed by his observations in Atlanta. "I have been compelled," he reported back, "to change my views very materially of the chance of the Southern manufacturer being rather more of a competitor than we are anxious to have."[15]

As the North turned to meet this challenge, many suggested emphasizing finer fabrics to avoid contending with southern mills running on coarse numbers. The *Boston Journal of Commerce* cautioned in 1883 that it would "not be many years before the majority of the heavy goods will be made in the South," and as a consequence New England would have "to go further with fine goods and fancy weaving."[16] The *Philadelphia Times* likewise maintained that "the eastern manufacturers have no permanent rem-

---

[13] *Address of Edward Atkinson of Boston, Massachusetts, Given in Atlanta, Georgia, in October, 1880 for the Promotion of an International Cotton Exposition* (Boston: A. Williams Co., 1881). See the preface to the pamphlet, written by Atkinson on January 13, 1881.

[14] *Bradstreet's*, November 26, 1881, p. 342.

[15] *Proceedings of the New England Cotton Manufacturers' Association*, October 26, 1881, p. 29.

[16] *Boston Journal of Commerce*, June 9, 1883, p. 90.

edy against this new competition, except in the manufacture of a finer and better finished grade of goods."[17] Many other spokesmen for the textile industry agreed that "the East will have to move toward higher things."[18]

These reflections stimulated some northerners to begin urging investment in educational institutions to provide the mechanical knowledge and skilled labor necessary for producing finer counts. They hoped to compete successfully with the more expensive European wares in the domestic market. Philadelphia manufacturers took the lead, and already in 1881 they were making plans for the establishment of a technical school in their city.[19] The undertaking received strong backing from the *Textile Record of America* and other influential sources in the area. And, in 1884, northern business interests happily announced the opening of the Philadelphia Textile School as part of their strategy to escape the growing threat from the South.

Northerners also responded to the southern mill boom by demanding tariff protection to help them acquire a larger share of the home market for fine goods. Senators Henry B. Anthony and Nelson W. Aldrich of Rhode Island headed the New England drive in 1883 to raise the duties on finer grades of cloth.[20] During special tariff hearings, northern factory owners explained their need for protection in terms of southern competition. One witness complained that "the Southern mills are driving New England into the manufacture of fine goods." Charles H. Dalton, a representative of the Arkwright Club of Boston, made the same point in his plea for high duties. "The increase of Southern spindles has been very large within the last two or three years," he testified, "and already several of the large factories in the North are beginning to abandon the manufacture of that class of goods."[21]

But most New England industrialists refused to surrender their interest in coarse cloth production without making a determined fight. Their attack plan involved the use of railway concessions as

---

[17] *Philadelphia Times*, as quoted in *Bradstreet's*, April 21, 1883, p. 247.

[18] *Textile Record of America*, November 1883, p. 291.

[19] *Bradstreet's*, January 20, 1881, p. 54.

[20] U.S., Congress, Senate, *Congressional Record*, 47th Cong., 2nd sess., February 2, 1883, 14, pt. 2: 1957–63.

[21] U.S., Congress, House, Committee on Ways and Means, *Arguments before the Committee of Ways and Means on the Morrison Tariff Bill*, 48th Cong., 1st sess., 1884, pp. 124, 171–72.

a weapon to defeat their southern enemies, especially in the contest for western markets. Northern dry goods representatives held an important conference in 1883 with the executive committee of the Pennsylvania, Baltimore and Ohio, New York Central, and Erie railroads. The textile directors made a strong appeal to the trunk lines for special rates on westbound traffic.[22] Yet the northern offensive did not frighten the members of the Southern Manufacturers' Association.[23] President H. H. Hickman later pointed out that his section possessed many advantages over the North in cotton manufacturing despite railroad freight rate discriminations favoring the Yankees.[24]

New Englanders understood that low cost labor gave the New South its key advantage. The *Boston Journal of Commerce*, for example, noted in 1882 that long hours and low wages provided the foundations for the southern textile industry: "These combined elements enter largely and are the most important factors that we have to contend with in the cost of production, and will be found the only real advantage the southern manufacturers have over us." The editors predicted that the exploitation of factory workers in the South would "undoubtedly be opposed in the near future by those who wish to be placed on equal terms in this important industry."[25] Though the big push for national labor legislation did not come for several years, New Englanders in the meantime devised a more subtle means to get at the root of the matter.

Hoping to raise labor costs in the South, Senator Henry W. Blair of New Hampshire introduced a bill in 1883 calling for federal appropriations to improve education, particularly in the southern states. "The labor of the South is cheap because it is ignorant," he explained later. "Make it intelligent and it will get what it is worth." Blair clearly tied his crusade for educational reform to the sectional struggle for dominance in the textile industry. "The question of the general education of the masses of the people, the masses of the producing element of the South," he emphasized, "is an absolute indispensable condition to the continuance of the prosperity of the capital and labor of the North." Blair hammered the point home. "There is no other protective system

---

[22] *Textile Record of America*, March 1883, pp. 61–62.
[23] *Textile Record of America*, April 1883, p. 105.
[24] *Boston Journal of Commerce*, January 12, 1889, p. 136.
[25] *Boston Journal of Commerce*, December 23, 1882, p. 98.

which can be applied to the great industrial system of the North in its competition with the developing industries of the South."[26]

The New Englanders also maneuvered in 1883 to raise the tariff on textile machinery in their effort to secure protection from the southern menace. Higher rates on imports made of iron and steel would make mill building more expensive and thereby retard industrial growth in areas lacking capital. Edward Atkinson privately briefed Nelson W. Aldrich a week before the Senate debate opened. "The chief obstacle to the extension of southern cotton manufacturing now consists in the heavy duties on iron and steel," he counselled, "the effect of which is to make the cost of cotton machinery about one third greater than it is in Europe."[27] Atkinson had acknowledged earlier that it was in the interest of the established manufacturers to have "a high duty on machinery."[28]

The debate in the Senate dramatized the sectional nature of the issue. John T. Morgan of Alabama charged that the proposed increase in machinery duties revealed the hypocrisy of the New Englanders "who profess to be willing to encourage American industry everywhere through this country." Morgan was angry. "Sir," he cried out, "there never was a more marked instance of sectional selfishness than that which is portrayed in this very movement."[29] Zebulon B. Vance of North Carolina had become equally impatient with Yankee rhetoric. "On all occasions the South is told that she ought to manufacture," he noted, adding that the time had arrived "to test the sincerity of those Senators in making those statements and in giving that advice." Vance called upon the northerners to match their words with deeds by abolishing rather than raising the levy on machinery used in cotton manufacturing.[30]

The New England political leaders assembled their forces to foil the southern counterattack. Senators William P. Frye of Maine, Justin S. Morrill of Vermont, and Nelson W. Aldrich of Rhode Island rose to defend the North's interests. They claimed that domestic machine shops were vital to the cotton industry and that

---

[26] U.S., Congress, Senate, *Congressional Record*, 50th Cong., 2nd sess., January 15, 1889, 20, pt. 1: 790–91.

[27] Edward Atkinson to Nelson W. Aldrich, January 22, 1883, Atkinson Letterbook, Massachusetts Historical Society, Boston.

[28] Edward Atkinson to David A. Wells, January 5, 1867, Atkinson Letterbook.

[29] U.S., Congress, Senate, *Congressional Record*, 47th Cong., 2nd sess., January 29, 1883, 14, pt. 2: 1729–30.

[30] Ibid., January 30, 1883, pp. 1764–65.

without adequate protection the machine makers would be forced to close down. They also discounted the argument that lower duties on textile equipment would speed the rise of factories in the South by compensating for the region's shortage of capital. Such reasoning failed to deceive their southern opponents, but the northerners succeeded in getting the desired hike in the tariff on cotton mill machinery.[31]

New England concern about industrial development in the New South corresponded with fluctuations in the business cycle. Northern anxiety declined as the downturn between 1884 and 1886 resulted in a sharp cutback in southern cotton mill building. Many small plants failed, and even some of the larger firms experienced financial difficulty. But the subsequent upswing between 1887 and 1892 brought another burst in the construction of textile enterprises in the southern piedmont. The clatter of the new spindles and looms running on coarse fabrics rang loudly in Yankee ears.

The cotton mill boom in the South reinforced earlier northern interest in manufacturing finer cloth. Commenting on southern industrial expansion in 1887, the *Springfield Union* could see no reason why Massachusetts textile companies "cannot make the grades of goods that are now imported."[32] *Bradstreet's*, which had quoted the *Union* in 1887, agreed two years later that New England manufacturers should give "more attention to the production of fine fabrics" in the struggle to hold their own against increasing pressure from the South.[33] The *Boston Journal of Commerce* expressed similar alarm about the rapid advances being made by southern cotton factories. "They are fast on the heels of the north," the editors admonished, "and the only way we at the north can lead the procession and run our mills at a profit is to get onto finer goods."[34]

A combination of factors intensified the impact of southern competition and produced a sense of crisis in New England during the last decade of the century. The great depression between 1893 and 1897 caused a painful drop in home demand for cotton goods. Northern factory construction slowed to a snail's pace, and the old established enterprises were forced to curtail production. Manage-

---

[31] Ibid., pp. 1769–79.

[32] *Springfield Union*, as quoted in *Bradstreet's*, August 13, 1887, p. 535.

[33] *Bradstreet's*, July 20, 1889, p. 455.

[34] *Boston Journal of Commerce*, May 9, 1891, p. 72.

ment did not suffer alone. Wage reductions and unemployment plagued the textile operatives and provoked labor unrest. To make conditions even more difficult, the southerners continued their mill building activity in full stride as their ability to vie successfully in overseas markets protected them from the worst consequences of the depression. By the end of the decade, southern factories were running more than a third as many cotton spindles as their New England rivals.[35]

The northern cotton manufacturers, in the meantime, were being harassed by state labor laws. The Massachusetts General Assembly passed an act in 1892 which effectively restricted work in textile factories to fifty-eight hours a week. The legislators in the Bay State even debated a fifty-four-hour labor bill in 1893, and many politicians continued to advocate more stringent measures in the following years.[36] Lawmakers in other New England states threatened to impose similar work regulations. This menacing agitation and actual legislation, combined with the glutted domestic market and the rising southern mills, provoked strong reactions in the North.

The large Massachusetts coarse cloth producers met stiff competition from their southern adversaries in foreign as well as domestic markets. The giant export mills in Lowell, for example, found themselves in serious trouble. Several of the best managed and most prosperous Lowell corporations responded to the situation by erecting branch factories in the South to make coarse fabrics for their overseas trade and by equipping their home plants to turn out finer goods for domestic consumption. Other Lowell export enterprises, not wanting to take on the expense of moving south, began to de-emphasize the manufacture of coarse cottons. The Appleton Manufacturing Company shifted part of its machinery to the production of specialties like blankets, while the Lawrence firm decided to close down its heavy sheeting department and to make nothing but hosiery.

As southern mill building continued during the depression decade, spokesmen for the New England textile industry stepped up their pleas for finer production. The *Boston Journal of Commerce*

---

[35] U.S., Department of Interior, *Twelfth Census of the United States*, 1900, Manufactures, 9, pt. 3: 46.

[36] John R. Commons, Ulrich B. Phillips, Eugene A. Gilmore, Helen L. Sumner, and John B. Andrews, eds., *A Documentary History of American Industrial Society* (Cleveland: Arthur H. Clark Co., 1909), p. 465.

repeatedly urged northern cotton manufacturers to climb the ladder to higher qualities in order to avoid being crushed by their southern antagonists.[37] The editors dismissed arguments that new machinery required for making finer numbers cost too much and advised mill owners to borrow the money because they could no longer afford to run on coarse counts.[38] "There is but one of two things," the editors exclaimed in 1895. "Northern cotton mills have got to make a high grade of goods, such as are imported largely at the present time, or else operate at a loss."[39]

The movement toward finer production strengthened the desire for tariff protection in the North. The Arkwright Club of Boston, which represented the most influential coarse cloth manufacturers in upper New England, began collecting data in 1893 to use in an effort to maintain high duties on cotton goods. The president of the organization explained that the information would be sent to Congressmen Thomas B. Reed and William F. Draper to help them "secure changes in the Wilson bill favorable to our special industries."[40] Producers of finer goods in lower New England likewise agitated the issue, and the *Boston Journal of Commerce* was pleased to report the results. "The new tariff bill is quite favorable to the fine-goods cotton industry," the editors rejoiced in 1894, "thanks to the able and capable work done at Washington by the Fall River manufacturers."[41]

Massachusetts industrialists also looked to education to aid them in their strategy of producing finer fabrics to evade southern competition. A northern business leader explained the need for technical education in simple language. "No amount of tariff legislation," he declared, "important as it is, can possibly preserve our home markets to our manufacturers unless they make the quality of things produced equal, if not superior, to that of their foreign competitor."[42] To help mill owners accomplish that objective, the Massachusetts General Assembly passed a law in 1895 authorizing the establishment of a textile school in any city having

---

[37] *Boston Journal of Commerce*, December 23, 1893, p. 184.

[38] *Boston Journal of Commerce*, September 15, 1894, p. 376.

[39] *Boston Journal of Commerce*, as quoted in *Bradstreet's*, March 23, 1895, p. 190.

[40] William C. Lovering to T. Jefferson Coolidge, December 5, 1893, Coolidge Papers, Massachusetts Historical Society, Boston.

[41] *Boston Journal of Commerce*, August 18, 1894, p. 312.

[42] *Dixie*, December 1899, p. 24.

more than 450,000 spindles and granting $25,000 in state aid on the condition that the municipality raise an equal amount. Lowell constructed a textile school a year later; and before the century ended, New Bedford and Fall River followed suit.[43]

By the middle of the decade, however, New England leaders had begun to realize that the strategy of turning to finer production to avoid southern competition possessed inherent difficulties. President William C. Lovering of the Arkwright Club noted in 1895 that "the average number of yarn spun at the South has been growing finer year by year." He also pointed out that "hardly 10 per cent of all the cotton goods consumed in this country could be classed as fine goods."[44] T. Jefferson Coolidge agreed that the production of finer cloth provided no easy solution to the problem caused by rivalry from the South. "The competition affects all kinds of goods manufactured in New England," Coolidge grumbled in 1896, "because if too many coarse goods are manufactured the mills here will be driven to fine goods, and then too many fine goods will be made."[45]

Massachusetts industrialists, recognizing the limitations involved in moving toward finer products, began to encourage the organization of southern mill hands. They wanted unions to raise the cost of labor in the South and thereby offset its chief competitive advantage. The *Boston Commercial Bulletin* urged trade unions to put southern textile workers on a par with those in Massachusetts. "If the national labor organizations really wish to aid, as they say they do," the editors proposed, "let them force, as they can force, a working week of not over fifty hours in every other state."[46] Senator Henry Cabot Lodge of Massachusetts agreed.

---

[43] Melvin T. Copeland, *The Cotton Manufacturing Industry of the United States* (Cambridge: Harvard University Press, 1912), pp. 135–37.

[44] *Manufacturers' Record*, January 25, 1895, p. 392; and *Chattanooga Tradesman*, April 15, 1895, p. 88.

[45] T. Jefferson Coolidge to Stephen O'Meara, April 6, 1896, Coolidge Letterbook, Massachusetts Historical Society, Boston. See also the *Twelfth Census of the United States*, 1900, Manufactures, 9, for Edward Stanwood's report on cotton manufacturing: "The fact that there is a great demand for coarse and medium . goods and a limited market for fine goods is pertinent to the suggestion that manufacturers who are unable to compete successfully in the production of standard plain cloths can find their salvation in turning to the spinning of fine yarns and the weaving of fine fabrics" (pt. 3: 39).

[46] *Boston Commercial Bulletin*, as quoted in Melton A. McLaurin, *Paternalism and Protest: Southern Cotton Mill Workers and Organized Labor* (Westport, Conn.: Greenwood Publishing, 1971), p. 130.

"The Southern operatives must be brought up to our standard," he wrote in 1898. "To this important work I hope our labor unions will address themselves."[47]

The American Federation of Labor had already entered the field in an effort to bring southern operatives into the National Union of Textile Workers. President Samuel Gompers played into the hands of the New England capitalists who were pointing to cheap labor in the South as an excuse for wage cuts in the North. "There are one of two alternatives which the Eastern textile workers now have," he reasoned in 1898: "either to support the textile workers of the South who are now in the struggle to either maintain or increase wages, or on the other hand for themselves to be compelled to enter into the struggle to prevent reductions in their own wages."[48] Gompers sent organizers into the southern states to make a major attempt to get child labor laws passed and thereby help protect northern operatives. But they toiled in vain in the late 1890s to improve working conditions in the southern textile industry.[49]

Experiments with black operatives in southern cotton factories helped repel the northern offensive. Aggravated by the activity of the National Union of Textile Workers, southern manufacturers used the threat of black labor to keep their white employees in line. John H. Montgomery explained in 1899 that success with black workers in his Vesta Cotton Mill in Charleston would mean "no more strikes, labor unions, etc. among the whites for fear that the Negro will step in and take their places." Other leading southern industrialists likewise regarded blacks as "a reserve force in case of strikes and labor troubles and combinations against capital."[50] The editors of *Dixie* agreed that "the negro stands as a permanent and positive barrier against labor organization in the South."[51]

Massachusetts cotton manufacturers, in the meantime, were struggling against labor reforms in their own state. Their fight

---

[47] Henry Cabot Lodge to George W. Poore, January 17, 1898, Lodge Letterbook, Massachusetts Historical Society, Boston. See also Lodge to Hayes, January 17, 1898.

[48] Samuel Gompers to H. S. Mills, January 6, 1898, Gompers Letterbook, Library of Congress, Washington, D.C.

[49] McLaurin, *Paternalism and Protest*, pp. 128–30, 141–42.

[50] Ibid., p. 64.

[51] *Dixie*, June 1899, p. 17.

began as soon as burdensome labor laws made themselves present in the early part of the decade. Prominent textile executives like Elliot C. Clarke and Howard Nichols appeared before special committees of the Massachusetts General Assembly to oppose pending legislation to shorten the work week.[52] "I simply want to give you a few cold facts in regard to Southern competition," Clarke thundered in 1892. "Southern mills are taking away my work from me, taking contracts from me."[53] Parroting the arguments of the proprietors, the *Boston Journal of Commerce* complained that labor laws were driving factories from the state.[54] The *Boston Commercial Bulletin* added its voice to the mounting protest and proclaimed that the time had come to say to the legislature—"Hands off our industries!"[55]

Massachusetts manufacturers applied even greater pressure on the general assembly as the depression sharpened the impact of southern rivalry.[56] William C. Lovering registered strong dissent in 1895 against further reductions in the hours of labor. "Our state is over-burdened with legislation," he lectured. "There is such a thing as being governed too much." T. Jefferson Coolidge agreed. "We have now got a load that we can hardly bear," he warned. "A straw may break us. Do not put that straw upon us."[57] Two years later, the Arkwright Club's *Report on Southern Competition* summarized the case for the mill owners. "The long hours run and the low wages paid," the report complained, "make the cost of labor in the South about 40 per cent less than in the North." It therefore

---

[52] *Manufacturers' Record*, April 11, 1891, p. 75; May 19, 1893, p. 292; *Boston Journal of Commerce*, May 13, 1893, p. 88; and *Chattanooga Tradesman*, May 15, 1892, p. 37.

[53] *Manufacturers' Record*, April 29, 1892, p. 34.

[54] *Boston Journal of Commerce*, December 22, 1894, p. 184; January 19, 1895; February 9, 1895.

[55] *Boston Commercial Bulletin*, as quoted in *Bradstreet's*, February 2, 1895, p. 78.

[56] An investigation by the Committee on Mercantile Affairs of the Massachusetts General Assembly inquiring into the reasons why cotton factories were leaving the state provided an opening for the mill owners to present their case against restrictive labor legislation: "This seems to be the year and this occasion the grand opportunity for a supreme effort to arrest the flood of onerous and burdensome legislation that has so long been setting against us." William C. Lovering to Howard Nichols, January 30, 1895, Dwight Manufacturing Company Papers, Baker Library, Harvard Business School, Boston.

[57] *Chattanooga Tradesman*, April 15, 1895, pp. 82–86.

urged the repeal of the fifty-eight-hour law in Massachusetts to lessen the labor-cost differences between the sections.[58]

The Committee on Labor in the Massachusetts Senate admitted in 1898 that cheap labor in the South was "a considerable factor" in causing depressed conditions in the Bay State. Rather than abolishing the fifty-eight-hour law, however, the committee believed that "other States should reduce their labor hours to the Massachusetts standard." As their solution to the problem of southern rivalry required strong action on the national rather than the state level, the committee members decided to leave the matter in the hands of their "fully advised" representatives in Washington. "It is agreed on all sides," the committee concluded, "that the National Congress should fix the hours of labor and in general control labor legislation, so that there may be uniformity in all the States."[59]

Massachusetts capitalists had already reached the same conclusion. "We need a national law controlling the hou.'s of labor," a Fall River manufacturer declared in 1895. "This is the chief solution to the problem of competition with the different sections of our country."[60] Others in Fall River agreed that "we should have a national law in regard to hours."[61] A Boston spinner likewise advocated national labor legislation in an address delivered in 1897 to the New England Cotton Manufacturers' Association. Since northerners could not "force the southern cotton operative to strike for higher wages," he reasoned, "it might be necessary to amend the Constitution" so that "prosperity in one part of the country may not be obtained by disaster in another."[62]

Representative William C. Lovering of Massachusetts brought this crucial question of sectional conflict into the national political arena. While still associated with the powerful Arkwright Club, he introduced a resolution in the House in January 1898 calling for an amendment to the Constitution which would authorize Con-

---

[58] The pamphlet was reprinted in *Manufacturers' Record*, December 24, 1897, pp. 338–39.

[59] U.S., Massachusetts, Legislature, Senate, *Report of the Committee on Labor*, No. 270 (May 18, 1898). The document was quoted in part by *Chattanooga Tradesman*, June 1, 1898, p. 58.

[60] *Boston Journal of Commerce*, February 2, 1895, p. 286.

[61] *Chattanooga Tradesman*, April 15, 1895, p. 86.

[62] *Transactions of the New England Cotton Manufacturers' Association*, April 28, 1897, p. 94.

gress to establish uniform hours of labor throughout the country.[63]
Lovering candidly admitted the motives behind his proposal a bit
later. "No state should be permitted to pass labor laws that would
give it an unequal chance in competition with neighboring states,"
he insisted. "The competition in cotton manufacturing is today so
sharp and the margin of profit so slender that the difference of a
few hours labor in a week in many instances constitutes a profit or
loss, as the case may be."[64]

The battle over the Lovering resolution came to a head during
the hearings conducted in February and March 1898 by the House
Judiciary Committee. The New England capitalists spoke through
their congressmen and their strange bedfellows in the American
Federation of Labor. Prior to his appearance before the committee,
Samuel Gompers explained that "every effort will be given toward
a successful result for the resolution."[65] The Southern Manufacturers' Association, on the other hand, sent a group of leading textile
executives to Washington to resist the northern attack. The southern defense mission, which included Ellison A. Smyth and Daniel
A. Tompkins, came prepared to use all available weapons in their
fight against the politics of social reform and the policy of internal
imperialism.

The southern mill managers even threatened to resort to the
widespread employment of black workers to intimidate their
northern antagonists. A business colleague advised Smyth to warn
the New Englanders that "if pushed" the southern manufacturers
would arm themselves with black operatives.[66] During the hearings, Tompkins made sure the Yankees got the message. If national
labor legislation forced a reduction of hours in the South, he
threatened, large numbers of blacks would be brought into the
cotton factories "because of the cheaper wages at which they will
be willing to work."[67] Such a course proved unnecessary. Despite the alliance between Gompers and the New Englanders, the

---

[63] U.S., Congress, House, *Congressional Record*, 55th Cong., 2nd sess., January
5, 1898, 31, pt. 1: 374.

[64] Record Group 233, Records of the U.S. House of Representatives, H.R.
55A-F19.3, National Archives, Washington, D.C.

[65] Samuel Gompers to Samuel Ross, March 1, 1898, Gompers Letterbook.

[66] Gustavus G. Williamson, Jr., "Cotton Manufacturing in South Carolina,
1865–1892" (Ph.D. dissertation, Johns Hopkins University, 1954), p. 178.

[67] Record Group 233, Records of the U.S. House of Representatives, H.R.
55A-F19.3, National Archives, Washington, D.C.

Lovering resolution met defeat in the Judiciary Committee. Few American businessmen were ready to open the way for federal interference with their labor practices.

Yet the Massachusetts cotton barons, who remained hostile to labor reforms in their own state, continued to advocate national labor laws. So did their political spokesmen.[68] And, a few months after the Lovering resolution was buried in committee, Congress passed an act creating the United States Industrial Commission. Section 3 of the act directed the organization to "furnish such information and suggest such laws as may be made a basis for uniform legislation by the various States of the Union."[69] The *Boston Journal of Commerce* happily announced that "the equalization of the hours of labor in the different States will be the leading feature of the investigation."[70]

Southerners responded by working hard to secure membership on the Industrial Commission in order to protect their sectional interest. A friend wrote Tompkins that "some good Southern representative, like yourself, who understands the labor situation in the South, should be on this Commission and combat what seems to be an effort on the part of other sections to establish hours of labor in the South by making them national and to our detriment."[71] Southerners succeeded in having Smyth appointed to the Commission, and when he retired Tompkins replaced him. Though the Commission did recommend that all the states in the country should adopt uniform labor laws, it concluded that national labor legislation would be unconstitutional.

This relationship between businessmen and reform represents a most significant episode in the long struggle for hegemony in the textile industry. The sectional conflict, which continued on into the twentieth century, had its root in the antebellum period when New England cotton manufacturers first began to fret about competition from Dixie. Their apprehensions diminished as southern attempts to throw off the shackles of a colonial economy met with

[68] U.S., Congress, House, *Congressional Record*, 56th Cong., 1st sess., April 30, 1900, 33, pt. 6: 4881–82.

[69] U.S., Congress, *Statutes at Large of the United States*, 55th Cong., 2nd sess., 1898, 30, p. 476.

[70] *Boston Journal of Commerce*, as quoted in *Dixie*, October 1898, p. 29.

[71] Howard B. Clay, "Daniel Augustus Tompkins: The Role of a New South Industrialist in Politics," *Studies in the History of the South*, vol. 3 (Greenville, S.C.: East Carolina College Publications in History, 1966), pp. 88–89.

frustration. But during the last two decades of the nineteenth century the New South's cotton mill campaign presented a serious threat to New England's prosperity. The response made by northern businessmen and politicians dramatized the wide gap between Yankee rhetoric and practice. Their reaction likewise confirmed the charges that New England leaders engaged in a concerted effort to retard southern industrial development.

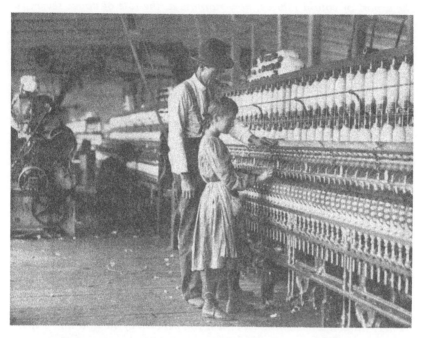

Courtesy of the International Museum of Photography at George Eastman House, Rochester, New York.

The export of cotton fabrics, now running at the rate of about seven per cent of our production, is the balance wheel on which the prosperity of the whole industry very much depends.
                              Edward Atkinson, Boston Industrialist, 1877

Once let our manufacturers taste the sweets of an augmenting foreign trade and their appetite will be as insatiable as the tiger's thirst for blood.
                                                        Lowell Times, 1887

As our cotton spindles increase in this country, and the competition between the northern and southern mills becomes more severe, the need of a foreign market for our cotton goods becomes more apparent.
                                          Boston Journal of Commerce, 1895

The recurrence of the periods of hard times may open our eyes to what we are able to do, and when we run our mills 20, 40, or 90 per cent of the time, we may think it advisable to run them 100 per cent of the time and give the export trade of this country the benefit.
                                                President Russel W. Eaton,
                            New England Cotton Manufacturers' Association, 1897

There can be no doubt that we have increased the number of our cotton mills far in excess of the domestic requirements and unless foreign markets are to be invaded by American cotton goods in volumes greatly exceeding the present it must necessarily follow that many millions of invested capital in this country will be put to great risk.
                                    American Wool and Cotton Reporter, 1900

I am an exporter. I want the world.
                        Charles L. Lovering, Massachusetts Cotton Manufacturer, 1901

7

New England's Export Orientation

New Englanders have traditionally engaged in long-distance trade in order to promote the wealth and welfare of their region. From the very beginning, the American colonists who settled along the North Atlantic coast depended upon maritime activity for their livelihood. The growing mercantile community developed a lucrative overseas business, and the consequent accumulation of capital gradually transformed Boston from a small commercial port into a great financial center. As shipping became less profitable in the early nineteenth century, Yankee merchants began to invest their savings in cotton manufacturing and related industrial ventures. But they did not abandon their export orientation. These ambitious entrepreneurs looked to foreign as well as domestic markets to absorb the output of their rising textile factories.

The Boston capitalists who built most of the mills in upper New England commenced exporting cotton cloth to Latin America and Asia as early as the 1820s.[1] They pushed especially hard to obtain an outlet in the Far East, and their sales to China increased rapidly after the Opium Wars made British merchandise less popular among the Orientals. The New England cotton manufacturers were shipping abroad almost 10 percent of their entire production by 1860, but shortages of the southern staple during the Civil War resulted in a drastic decline in their overseas commerce. The English factory owners seized the opportunity to strengthen their

---

[1] Caroline F. Ware, *Early New England Cotton Manufacture: A Study in Industrial Beginnings* (New York: Russell and Russell, 1966), pp. 189–97.

grip on the cotton goods trade of the world by adapting some of their machinery to run on the cheap Surat fiber grown in India. Nevertheless, the farsighted Boston industrialists took advantage of the idle period to expand their spindle capacity, and during the three decades following the war they struggled to regain their foreign trade.

The New England cotton textile industry emerged in the last third of the nineteenth century as two separate systems of operation characterized by different product lines and marketing practices. A high proportion of the spinning and weaving factories were concentrated below Cape Cod in the tidewater area between Providence and Fall River where climatic conditions encouraged the manufacture of medium and fine fabrics. These locally owned enterprises sold the great bulk of their prints and fancier goods in the domestic market. On the other hand, the mills situated along the Merrimac River from Lawrence to Manchester and their sister establishments farther up the Atlantic seaboard devoted most of their spindles and looms to the production of coarse yarn and cloth. These Boston controlled corporations sent large quantities of heavy sheetings and drills to foreign markets.

The downswing in the business cycle between 1873 and 1878 spurred New England cotton manufacturers to redouble their efforts to recapture the export trade they had lost during the war. At first, mill managers reacted to the sudden drop in home demand by urging limitations in output. The treasurers of the larger factories held two key meetings in Boston and Providence in 1874 and adopted resolutions calling for the curtailment of production by at least a third.[2] As the depression became more severe, however, the lords of the loom turned their attention to outside markets. Companies in upper New England which emphasized the manufacture of coarse fabrics tried to increase their foreign sales. Even firms in lower New England making a less suitable class of goods for export were often driven into dumping their surplus products overseas. Hence the amount of cloth sold abroad rose sharply. The average annual value of American cotton textile exports stood at little over three million dollars between 1870 and 1875. During the next five-year period, however, the average swelled more than threefold.[3]

The *New York Commercial and Financial Chronicle* diagnosed

---

[2] Victor S. Clark, *The History of Manufactures in the United States*, vol. 2 (New York: McGraw-Hill, 1929), p. 404.

[3] U.S., Department of Commerce and Labor, *Statistical Abstract of the United States*, 1910, p. 491.

New England's ills in terms of domestic overproduction and persistently asserted that the only remedy lay in foreign trade. "Production must either be decreased or our own circle of consumers enlarged," the editors declared in 1874. Finding the first alternative unacceptable, they advised cotton manufacturers to prepare themselves to vie for "the markets of the world."[4] The eminent business journal made the same analysis of the situation two years later. "Our power to consume cotton has outstripped our capacity for consuming goods," the editors explained. Painful though it was, they hoped that the difficulty would provoke mill owners to engage in "a successful competition with other countries in the markets of the world."[5]

Boston textile executives, like Edward Atkinson, agreed that overseas economic expansion provided the most attractive way to end the hardships caused by the contraction of the domestic market. Such reasoning prompted Atkinson to deliver a major paper, "The Export Trade in Cotton Goods and the Means of Its Promotion," before the New England Cotton Manufacturers' Association in 1876. He concluded his presentation by predicting that an increase in textile exports would help bring good times back to New England.[6] In the same year, Atkinson influenced several factory owners to display samples of their wares in the principal cloth consuming countries around the world. He also induced many cotton manufacturers to petition the American government to take steps to stop the British from imitating their trademarks in foreign countries.[7]

Atkinson maintained his agitation in behalf of enlarging the marketplace for textile products as the economic adversity persisted. "The export of cotton fabrics," he wrote Secretary of State William M. Evarts in 1877, "now running at the rate of about seven per cent of our production, is the balance wheel on which the prosperity of the whole industry very much depends."[8] After the lean years finally passed, Atkinson reminded his business friends in a special report for the Census Bureau in 1880 that foreign

---

[4] *New York Commercial and Financial Chronicle*, November 21, 1874, p. 517.

[5] *New York Commercial and Financial Chronicle*, January 1876, p. 5.

[6] *Proceedings of the New England Cotton Manufacturers' Association*, April 26, 1876, pp. 33–63.

[7] Harold F. Williamson, *Edward Atkinson: The Biography of an American Liberal, 1827–1905* (Cambridge, Mass.: Riverside Press, 1934), p. 37.

[8] Edward Atkinson to William M. Evarts, April 13, 1877, Atkinson Letterbook, Massachusetts Historical Society, Boston.

commerce had constituted "a most important element in the returning prosperity of our cotton mills." Though some small overseas shipments had been sold below cost, he explained, most of the coarse sheetings and drills sent to Asia, Africa, and Latin America had been made by "strong and prosperous corporations paying regular dividends."[9]

The export movement launched during the depression led northern textile spokesmen to advocate government subsidies for the American merchant marine.[10] They believed that cheaper transportation facilities would help factory masters outmaneuver their British rivals in the Latin American trade. A member of the New England Cotton Manufacturers' Association urged his colleagues in 1878 to use whatever influence they had to persuade Congress to appropriate funds for steamship lines connecting the United States with "the enormous market open to our manufactures in South America."[11] Some New England political leaders were quick to take the cue. Senator Henry W. Blair, for example, demanded shipping subsidies in 1879 to "open a direct trade with South America."[12] These proposals failed as prosperity returned, but most politicians who refused to grant money to the merchant marine had not lost interest in tapping distant markets. They merely wanted to employ different means to accomplish the same ends.

Standard accounts have concluded that the upswing in the business cycle between 1879 and 1883 drew cotton manufacturers away from foreign trade.[13] A closer examination of the available evidence, however, makes it clear that such an interpretation greatly oversimplifies the matter. Although American cotton textile exports did decrease in value from $11,438,660 in 1878 to $9,981,418 in 1880, this downward trend soon reversed itself.[14]

---

[9] U.S., Department of Interior, *Tenth Census of the United States*, 1880, Manufactures, 8, pt. 2: 12.

[10] See, for example, *New York Commercial and Financial Chronicle*, February 24, 1877, pp. 167–69; June 30, 1877, p. 601; and *Bradstreet's*, October 8, 1879, p. 2; November 1, 1879, p. 5.

[11] *Proceedings of the New England Cotton Manufacturers' Association*, April 24, 1878, p. 49.

[12] U.S., Congress, Senate, *Congressional Record*, 45th Cong., 3rd sess., February 28, 1879, 8, pt. 3: 2121–22.

[13] Melvin T. Copeland, *The Cotton Manufacturing Industry of the United States* (Cambridge: Harvard University Press, 1912), p. 221; and Clark, *The History of Manufactures in the United States*, 2: 415.

[14] *Statistical Abstract of the United States*, 1910, p. 491.

Overseas shipments climbed in value to $13,571,387 in 1881, and consular reports hailed the increased sales in various foreign countries.[15] Uncolored cloth exports, furthermore, jumped in value by $3,063,582 between 1879 and 1882, while colored cargoes dipped by $882,966.[16] Since plain gray and white lots consisted of rough material, these figures indicate that, as exports of finer fabrics declined somewhat, foreign sales of coarse goods made significant gains.

A tendency to generalize what happened in lower New England to the rest of the textile industry has distorted secondary studies. Many establishments in this locale did turn back to the domestic market in response to high prices at home and a lack of demand for medium and fine cloth abroad. Yet numerous enterprises in upper New England (like their counterparts in the southern states) continued to export large quantities of coarse fabrics during these flourishing years. As the *Boston Commercial Bulletin* noted in 1882, several big Massachusetts cotton mills were running "almost exclusively" on heavy sheetings and drills for shipment overseas.[17] The fact that a great many thriving corporations maintained their export trade contradicts the idea that during periods of prosperity the home market always afforded better prices for all kinds of cotton goods produced in every part of the country.

New England's success in exporting coarse cloth in the early 1880s gave rise to dreams of dislodging Great Britain from its dominant position in the China market. Business journals and consular reports repeatedly boasted that the Chinese people preferred unadulterated American cottons to highly sized fabrics made in England.[18] Northern publications, like the *Boston Commercial Bulletin*, made their readers familiar with "the story of American cotton goods, such as drills and heavy sheetings, successfully competing with the starch, china-clay, terra alba stuffed English article."[19] The American consul in Tientsin expressed the prevailing spirit of optimism. He predicted that the practice of exporting pure cotton fabrics "would result in the ascendancy of American

---

[15] U.S., Department of State, *Consular Report* No. 19 (May 1882), pp. 6–7.

[16] *Statistical Abstract of the United States*, 1910, p. 491.

[17] *Boston Commercial Bulletin*, as quoted in *Bulletin of the American Iron and Steel Association*, February 1, 1882, p. 33.

[18] See, for example, *Bradstreet's*, November 22, 1897, p. 4; March 12, 1881, p. 149; May 6, 1882, p. 273; and May 27, 1882, p. 324.

[19] *Boston Commercial Bulletin*, as quoted in *Bulletin of the American Iron and Steel Association*, November 10, 1880, p. 277.

interests, and a complete reversing of the present huge and unnatural disproportion between American and English trade in China."[20]

These delightful prospects, however, seemed threatened in 1882 when California politicians, responding to the pleas of labor unions, introduced bills into the Congress to prohibit immigration from China. A desire for more customers, not what they considered coolie operatives, led New England textile interests to oppose these schemes. They feared that an exclusionist law would alienate the Asians and thereby jeopardize their Far Eastern commerce. Massachusetts congressmen and senators were particularly vocal in their dissent. They agreed with Representative William W. Rice of Worcester that immigration restrictions imposed on Orientals "would shut the doors of China to American influence and American trade."[21] Against their protests, Congress adopted an exclusionist policy. New England business circles worried that the Chinese would retaliate at once, but they did not organize a boycott against American goods until after the end of the century.[22]

The decline in the business cycle between 1884 and 1886 provided a more immediate menace to the New England textile industry. Profits fell, mills closed, and unemployment rose. At various times, a high percentage of cotton spindles remained inactive as factory managers independently cut back production when they could not agree upon a common program of curtailment. "There is a general depression throughout the country," a representative of the Arkwright Club of Boston complained. "We feel it severely in fabrics."[23] As the downward spiral continued, the atmosphere of confidence that had surrounded the business disappeared. The *New York Commercial and Financial Chronicle* reported that the summer of 1885 was "about the darkest period the cotton goods trade ever experienced in this country."[24]

The economic slump did not have the same effect on all segments of the textile industry. The stagnation of the home market particularly hurt the medium and fine cloth manufacturers cen-

---

[20] U.S., Department of State, *Consular Report* No. 12 (June 1881), p. 301.

[21] U.S., Congress, House, *Congressional Record*, 47th Cong., 1st sess., March 15, 1882, 13, pt. 2: 1939.

[22] *Boston Journal of Commerce*, July 8, 1882, p. 111.

[23] U.S., Congress, House, *Arguments before the Committee of Ways and Means on the Morrison Tariff Bill*, 48th Cong., 1st sess., 1884, p. 129.

[24] *New York Commercial and Financial Chronicle*, September 11, 1886, p. 295.

tered in southern New England. Some were willing to export at a loss in an attempt to secure a temporary vent for their large accumulation of stock. While firms in the Providence and Fall River area suffered, a few notable establishments producing coarse fabrics in northern New England basked in prosperity. The giant Pepperell and Laconia enterprises operating in Maine, for instance, remained able to pay handsome dividends during the hard times. These two mills were selling more than half of their total output in Asia, the *Lewiston Journal* explained in 1885, "and this is where they make their money."[25]

The New Englanders became increasingly interested in foreign commerce as the depression deepened. *Bradstreet's* correspondent in Boston regarded the export demand for cotton goods as an "escape valve" for domestic overproduction. The editors agreed that "a paying foreign market would counterbalance the commercial depression at home."[26] The *Boston Journal of Commerce* criticized New England cotton manufacturers for ignoring the export trade during years of prosperity and advised them to seek external markets in order to avoid periodic business troubles.[27] The editors believed that a growing demand from abroad "would keep their mills running all the time, enable them to pay satisfactory dividends, and keep labor contented because well employed."[28] And the *Lowell Times* applauded when local textile enterprises expanded their overseas sales. "Once let our manufacturers taste the sweets of an augmenting foreign trade," the editors predicted, "and their appetite will be as insatiable as the tiger's thirst for blood."[29]

Despite these expectations, the export trade in cotton textiles experienced a serious setback shortly after the domestic economy recovered. This was due in part to the fact that spinners of prints and finer fabrics in lower New England stopped dumping abroad. The *Boston Journal of Commerce* explained that overseas business was no longer energetically solicited because the home market was

---

[25] *Lewiston Journal*, as quoted in *Boston Journal of Commerce*, February 14, 1885, p. 176.

[26] *Bradstreet's*, October 11, 1884, pp. 225, 228.

[27] *Boston Journal of Commerce*, October 25, 1884, p. 20; September 19, 1885, p. 224.

[28] *Boston Journal of Commerce*, March 21, 1885, p. 230.

[29] *Lowell Times*, as quoted in *Boston Journal of Commerce*, September 10, 1887, pp. 214–15.

absorbing cotton goods "at more remunerative prices."[30] *Brad-street's* likewise attributed the reduction in foreign sales to "the general buoyancy of the domestic market."[31] But the export lull had more to do with floods and famine in China than with economic conditions inside the United States. A sudden drop in Oriental demand was primarily responsible for the sharp decline in textile exports. American shipments of uncolored cloth to China decreased in value from $5,181,050 to $1,203,540 between 1887 and 1890, and as a result total exports of plain gray and white material simultaneously fell from $9,256,486 to $5,480,403.[32]

The fluctuations in the China trade during the economic revival between 1887 and 1892 demonstrated the importance of foreign markets for the factories making rough fabrics in upper New England. The dragging Asian demand depressed the coarse goods branch of the industry, while the producers of higher quality textiles enjoyed a brisk domestic business. Yet these circumstances were soon reversed. American sales of uncolored cloth to China climbed back in value to $5,321,500 in 1891, and total exports of plain cloth jumped again to $9,277,112.[33] At the same time, the domestic market for prints and finer fabrics became sluggish. The consequences were immediately felt. "The cotton mills which at present are reported in the best condition are those which manufacture principally for export," *Bradstreet's* noted in 1891. "Those which produce goods for home consumption solely are not doing so well."[34]

The rapid rise of cotton factories in the New South, however, presented a serious menace to the coarse goods manufacturers in upper New England. Several leading corporations in Lowell responded to the distressing situation in the 1890s by migrating southward. The Massachusetts, Boott, Whittier, and Merrimack enterprises all erected branch factories in the cotton states to make coarse cloth for export. These mills possessed valuable trademarks because of their long-standing policy of shipping pure cottons to foreign countries; but they were encountering stiff competition

[30] *Boston Journal of Commerce*, June 9, 1888, p. 84.

[31] *Bradstreet's*, May 18, 1889, p. 311.

[32] U.S., Treasury Department, Bureau of Statistics, *Monthly Summary of Imports and Exports of the United States*, n.s., 1, 1893–94, p. 678.

[33] Ibid.

[34] *Bradstreet's*, June 6, 1891, p. 357.

from their southern adversaries, particularly in the China market. Their decision to move south centered on the crucial labor question. Unable to persuade the Massachusetts General Assembly to repeal the statute limiting factory work to fifty-eight hours a week in the Bay State, these firms hoped to exploit the large supply of cheap and tractable labor in the South and thereby maintain their overseas commerce.

Representatives of the giant Massachusetts Mills, which had been the largest export establishment in the country, explained in clear language why they elected to build a factory in Georgia. Agent William S. Southworth pointed out that the Lowell company had been "losing to its Southern competitors the export trade to China, which it had had for so many years and must keep in order to pay any returns."[35] A bit later, Treasurer Charles L. Lovering noted that he and his associates had been "forced to recognize that we could not make goods in Lowell and export them at a profit." The home plant in Massachusetts was handicapped by high wages and short hours, he continued, but the firm was still able to take advantage of its popular trademarks by shipping abroad large amounts of coarse goods produced in its Georgia branch. "I am an exporter," Lovering concluded bluntly. "I want the world."[36]

The great depression between 1893 and 1897, in the meantime, intensified the impact of southern competition and produced a sense of crisis in New England. The northern textile industry experienced declining profits, wage reductions, periodic curtailment, and labor unrest. Despite the glut in the home market, the New South continued its mill building program at full speed. The number of active cotton spindles in the four leading southern states increased by more than 200 percent during the last decade in the century, while the rate of population growth in the United States lagged far behind.[37] These harsh facts led more and more northern cotton manufacturers to believe that the American market could no longer consume the output of their mills. Apart from their un-

[35] *Manufacturers' Record*, April 1, 1898, p. 169.

[36] U.S., Congress, House, Industrial Commission on the Relations of Capital and Labor, Report, *House Document* No. 183, 57th Cong., 1st sess., 1901, pp. 529–33.

[37] U.S., Department of Interior, *Twelfth Census of the United States*, 1900, Manufactures, 9, pt. 3: 46.

successful attempt to stifle southern industrial development, the New Englanders looked to foreign markets to find a remedy for their domestic troubles.

The *Boston Journal of Commerce* initiated a vigorous campaign in 1894 to encourage northern manufacturers to seek overseas markets for their surplus fabrics. The paper repeatedly compared the busy factories in the South with the silent spindles in New England, holding up the contrast as an object lesson in the value of foreign commerce. The editors noted that while "many large and long established cotton mills in the north have had to curtail their production largely, and some to stop entirely, the manufacturers in the south, except in very few instances, have operated their mills on full time."[38] The editors argued persistently that the export trade made the difference. "There are very few who realize the amount of goods that is sent abroad by our southern cotton mills," they asserted, "and to this, perhaps as much as any other one thing, can be attributed their success."[39]

Despite its desire to promote investment in manufacturing, the *Journal of Commerce* soon admitted its growing fear of domestic overproduction. "As our cotton spindles increase in this country, and the competition between the northern and southern mills becomes more severe, the need of a foreign market for our cotton goods becomes more apparent," the editors warned in 1895. "We shall soon be in a condition to manufacture more cotton goods than we can use in this country, and shall be obliged to have an outlet for them."[40] A year later, the paper advocated a sustained policy of overseas economic penetration to avoid the effects of the business cycle. "Spasmodic efforts to get rid of surplus goods in years of overproduction," the editors insisted, "should give way to persistent efforts to extend our markets as a co-ordinate branch of the industry regardless of surplus stocks."[41]

Several papers read before the New England Cotton Manufacturers' Association likewise advocated expansion abroad as the best solution to the problem of overproduction at home. "The

---

[38] *Boston Journal of Commerce*, December 29, 1894, p. 200.

[39] *Boston Journal of Commerce*, May 12, 1894, p. 88. See also June 16, 1894, p. 168; July 7, 1894, p. 216; and July 13, 1895, p. 232.

[40] *Boston Journal of Commerce*, March 23, 1895, p. 392.

[41] *Boston Journal of Commerce*, October 10, 1896, p. 24.

rapid development of the manufacture of cotton goods in the South has created new problems which must be solved, and the home market is not able to absorb the output of the old and new mills," one speaker declared in 1897. "The most important matter which calls for the consideration of the cotton mill owners of the United States at the present time is the expansion of the export trade." President Russell W. Eaton urged the members of the association to remember what had been said and then added his own comments. "The recurrence of the periods of hard times may open our eyes to what we are able to do," Eaton hoped, "and when we run our mills 20, 40, or 90 per cent of the time, we may think it advisable to run them 100 per cent of the time and give the export trade of this country the benefit."[42]

Another speaker in 1897 agreed that foreign commerce provided the surest road away from domestic crisis. "In many lines of goods the existing manufacturing establishments can produce a vast amount more than what the United States can consume," he noted, and southern factories "can undersell or compete easily with the eastern mills on medium and coarse fabrics." Realizing that a changeover to finer cloth provided no gate of escape, he believed that only one option remained open. "Suffice to say," he concluded, "that the large number of old concerns in New England are in a much better position to consider the advisability of manufacturing some cotton goods for export, than they are for manufacturing very fine fabrics for the home market."[43]

Addressing the New England Cotton Manufacturers' Association in 1898, Christopher P. Brooks reiterated the expansionist arguments. Brooks was the director of the Lowell Textile School, which had been built as part of the North's strategy of making finer goods to avoid competition from the South. Yet he had come to believe that the rapid construction of cotton factories had resulted "in a greater production than this country can consume," and he reasoned that "an efficient remedy would be in an increased export trade."[44] Everyone agreed. A few months later, by a unanimous vote, the members of the association established a commit-

---

[42] *Transactions of the New England Cotton Manufacturers' Association*, October 28, 1897, pp. 111–12.

[43] Ibid., pp. 284–85.

[44] *Transactions of the New England Cotton Manufacturers' Association*, April 28, 1898, p. 228.

tee to study the ways and means available for promoting foreign commerce.[45]

Northern trade journals concerned with the textile industry also subscribed to the theory that domestic overproduction made foreign markets imperative. "Must we not accept the conclusion that home consumption cannot take the product of our mills running on full time?" the *New York Commercial and Financial Chronicle* asked in 1897. "In other words, do not the developments of the past few years disclose a situation in the cotton goods industry which makes it necessary that we cultivate foreign markets or else do as we have done the past two years, alternate full time with short time while accepting as chronic conditions a dragging market, small profits and disgruntled labor?"[46]

Other leading business publications in the North similarly defined the situation confronting cotton manufacturers in either/or terms. The dry goods editor of the *New York Journal of Commerce and Commercial Bulletin* could see only two different ways to meet the challenge posed by the onslaught of domestic overproduction. "The cotton industry must find markets abroad," he assumed in early 1898, "or else tear down the old mills and wipe out the capital invested in the least effective plants, and limit the output to what the United States can consume."[47] The choice was obvious. A few months later, the editor repeated his analysis of the ills plaguing the textile industry. "We must," he concluded, "find our markets to a very much larger extent outside our own country."[48]

The *Textile Record of America* stood almost alone in denying the validity of the overproduction thesis. The Philadelphia paper represented the manufacturers of finer fabrics in the Middle Atlantic states who were primarily interested in protecting their domestic trade. In line with their home market orientation, the editors argued that underconsumption rather than overproduction had caused the depression. "At this very moment there are many hundreds of thousands of Americans, in all parts of the country, who cannot afford to buy cloth enough to cover their nakedness," the editors pointed out in a revealing comment on the malfunc-

---

[45] *Transactions of the New England Cotton Manufacturers' Association*, September 28, 1898, p. 78.

[46] *New York Commercial and Financial Chronicle*, December 25, 1897, p. 1196.

[47] *New York Journal of Commerce and Commercial Bulletin*, as quoted in *Boston Journal of Commerce*, February 5, 1898, p. 269.

[48] *Manufacturers' Record*, April 22, 1898, p. 221.

tioning of the political economy. "The real trouble, then, is not at all that the mill-product is in excess of any possible demand, but very decidedly that the demand is not presented, and therefore the mills cannot sell, because great armies of our own fellow-citizens are too poor to buy."[49]

The producers of medium and fine cottons in lower New England, however, never advocated a radical change in the capitalist system designed to achieve an internal balance between supply and demand. Instead, like coarse goods manufacturers throughout the nation, they turned their attention to foreign markets in a search for a more conservative solution to their domestic problem. Besides supporting the drive to enlarge the marketplace for rough fabrics, they hoped to ship finer cloth abroad. The Fall River Board of Trade, for example, urged Secretary of State John Hay to negotiate a reciprocity treaty with Canada in an attempt to help local cotton mill owners increase their sales in that country.[50]

A widespread belief that foreign commerce had helped pull the cotton industry out of the depression reinforced the already strong export commitment. The *Textile World* credited the return of prosperity in late 1898 to the growing overseas demand for coarse cloth. "We have open to us a great field in which to work in this direction," the editors remarked, "the necessity of which we are more keenly alive to than ever before."[51] Edward Stanwood summarized these sentiments in his report on the cotton industry in the census of 1900. "The existence of an important outlet for such goods," he noted, "saved manufacturers from a disastrous glut, and mitigated the keenness of the competition that became most serious when the South entered the market as a great producer."[52]

The traumatic encounter with the great depression convinced almost everyone associated with the textile industry that export markets were essential for the continued well-being of New England. The *Boston Journal of Commerce* carried editorial after editorial warning that cotton mill owners must cultivate overseas trade in order to prevent the recurrence of hard times.[53] "Owing

---

[49] *Textile Record of America*, January 1898, p. 9.

[50] Josich Brown to John Hay, July 20, 1899, Record Group 59, Miscellaneous Letters, Department of State, National Archives, Washington, D.C.

[51] *Textile World*, November 1898, p. 32.

[52] *Twelfth Census of the United States*, 1900, Manufactures, 9, pt. 3: 21.

[53] *Boston Journal of Commerce*, October 21, 1899, p. 70; April 14, 1900, p. 50; and July 28, 1900, p. 354.

to our past experience," President D. M. Thompson of the New England Cotton Manufacturers' Association explained in 1900, "a feeling exists that over-production is an eminent peril, a source of constant danger." He shared the common conviction that the quick pace of cotton factory construction made "the acquisition of foreign markets a vital necessity."[54]

New England textile spokesmen maintained their expansionist outlook as business conditions continued to improve at the turn of the century. "There can be no doubt that we have increased the number of our cotton mills far in excess of the domestic requirements," the *American Wool and Cotton Reporter* warned in 1900, "and unless foreign markets are to be invaded by American cotton goods in volumes greatly exceeding the present it must necessarily follow that many millions of invested capital in this country will be put to great risk."[55] In the same year, a speaker reminded the members of the New England Cotton Manufacturers' Association that social stability as well as financial security depended upon foreign trade because in America "the contented worker must be the busy worker."[56]

These New England cotton manufacturers had been engaged in overseas economic expansion throughout the last third of the nineteenth century. It is true that the producers of medium and fine fabrics below Cape Cod exhibited only a sporadic interest in foreign commerce during the 1870s and 1880s. But the coarse cloth makers operating above Boston sustained their involvement in long-distance trade regardless of the fluctuations in the business cycle. Then, in the 1890s, an expansionist consensus emerged, as more and more northern textile leaders came to the conclusion that domestic overproduction made external markets vitally important to the prosperity and tranquility of their entire region. Hence, despite the shift from commerce to industry, New Englanders remained committed to their export orientation.

---

[54] *Transactions of the New England Cotton Manufacturers' Association*, April 25, 1900, pp. 89–90.

[55] *American Wool and Cotton Reporter*, as quoted in *Chattanooga Tradesman*, July 1, 1900, p. 58.

[56] *Transactions of the New England Cotton Manufacturers' Association*, April 25, 1900, pp. 180–82.

Courtesy of the Graniteville mill, Graniteville, South Carolina.

We have reached that point in the development of the cotton industry where we make more goods than the markets which we now have will take. . . . The measures of relief are the same for both sections. The relief can best be brought about by the co-operation of all who are engaged in cotton manufacture in the United States.

Daniel A. Tompkins, North Carolina Textile Executive, May 1898

We the undersigned Cotton Manufacturers and Merchants interested in the exporting of textile goods to China, respectfully call your attention to the critical conditions confronting our trade in that Empire. . . . Unless a vigorous policy is pursued on the part of the United States Government, these markets will be eventually closed to our trade.

Petition to Secretary of State John Hay, January 1899

A large number of the mills in this state are making goods for the China or Eastern trade. If by any chance this demand should be cut off, the mills would be compelled to shut down, or to get into direct competition with the other mills which are making goods for home consumption. You can at once see what the importance of the China trade is to us; it is everything.

South Carolina Mill Owners' Petition to Their Congressmen for an Open Door Policy, September 1899

If you want the 'open door,' the United States now holds the key. The archipelago of the Philippines. . . . The control of them, or at least of some portions, is the only safeguard for our trade interests in the East.

Reply of Senator John L. McLaurin of South Carolina to the Mill Owners, October 1899

We believe it is the duty of all good citizens of the United States to support the present administration in its efforts to protect our treaty rights in China, and if they have to send troops from Manila or from San Francisco to do so, it should be done.

Richmond Times, July 1900

The undersigned manufacturers of cotton goods in the Southern States desire to express approval of the policy of the government in the protection of American interests in China, known as the 'open door' policy, and trust that this position may be maintained.

Memorial to Secretary of State John Hay, November 1900

8

Sectional Reunion and Informal Empire

*D*uring the last third of the nineteenth century, the New South and New England engaged in a bitter contest for dominance in the American textile industry. A broad consensus in the southern states, including rural and urban elements, sponsored a cotton mill campaign as the first step in a long struggle to overhaul their entire economy and overcome their colonial status. Yankee business interests and their political representatives responded to the challenge by proposing various measures designed to impede the rise of cotton factories in the South. But the continuation of this sectional conflict did not prevent northerners and southerners from joining forces in an outburst of economic nationalism. And, as the century came to a close, these old domestic adversaries demanded for their mutual benefit an aggressive foreign policy.

The great depression between 1893 and 1897 set the stage for sectional reunification in an attempt to influence the shaping of American diplomacy. The contraction of the internal market, combined with the rapid industrial expansion in the South, generated a widespread belief that the country could manufacture more yarn and cloth than it could consume. Almost everyone connected with the textile business agreed that long-distance trade provided the only acceptable solution to the problem of overproduction at home. Southerners, armed with a large supply of cheap and docile labor, were better equipped than northerners to obtain a vent for their surplus cotton goods. Thus, as the depression deepened, they developed an extensive overseas commerce, particularly in northern China and Manchuria.

New England textile spokesmen began to link the welfare of their own region to the New South's ability to compete successfully in the markets of the world. Noting that foreign countries were purchasing large quantities of southern cloth, the *Boston Commercial Bulletin* hoped in 1895 that "the expansion of this export demand may ease the pressure from southern looms."[1] The *Boston Journal of Commerce* made the same analysis of the situation a few years later. The editors regarded production cutbacks and wage reductions as "temporary makeshifts" and argued that permanent prosperity depended upon the opening of external markets for cotton fabrics. "It perhaps makes no difference whether the southern or the northern manufacturers get these new markets, in so far as the general result is concerned," the editors reasoned, "for if the south should go abroad the north could remain at home in comfort."[2]

American cotton manufacturers maintained their keen interest in foreign markets during the flourishing years following the upturn of the business cycle in 1898. They were convinced that their exports of heavy sheetings, shirtings, and drills had enabled them to survive past difficulties. They also believed that continued overseas shipments of coarse fabrics would help them endure the onslaught of hard times in the future. Southerners wanted to enlarge the marketplace to underwrite the prosperous operation of already existing establishments and to make room for the construction of many more textile enterprises. Northerners hoped that an increasing foreign trade would absorb the output of the southern mills and allow their own factories to find enough customers in the domestic market.

Daniel A. Tompkins played a central role in uniting American cotton manufacturers behind a drive to establish a far-flung seaborne empire. Like other southern industrialists and their agrarian allies, he looked to foreign commerce to stimulate cotton mill building and thereby create a local demand for farm produce. The conviction that the whole New South program for economic development required a constantly expanding marketplace spurred Tompkins to become a vigorous imperial crusader. He wrote pamphlets, delivered speeches, and corresponded with prominent politicians in an effort to demonstrate that domestic overproduction made foreign outlets for textile wares a vital necessity.[3] He

---

[1] *Boston Commercial Bulletin*, as quoted in *Bradstreet's*, January 26, 1895, p. 62.

[2] *Boston Journal of Commerce*, January 15, 1898, p. 248.

[3] Daniel A. Tompkins, *American Commerce, Its Expansion: A Collection of Addresses and Pamphlets Relating to the Extension of Foreign Markets for American*

also worked closely with business leaders throughout the country to get the national government to help protect and extend his section's export trade.

As the president of the Southern Cotton Spinners' Association, Tompkins directed a movement for reconciliation at home in order to promote expansion abroad. He reminded the members of the organization in 1898 that "we have reached that point in the development of the cotton industry where we make more goods than the markets which we now have will take." Tompkins dismissed the alternative of making internal adjustments to achieve a balance between supply and demand. "Curtailment of production can bring only the most temporary and unsatisfactory relief," he maintained, while overseas sales offered an attractive and lasting cure for the domestic ills plaguing the textile business. "The measures of relief are the same for both sections," he insisted. Thus northern and southern factory managers should "join together to procure the necessary legislation from congress to improve our trade."[4]

Tompkins reiterated his argument for economic nationalism in a speech before the Southern Cotton Spinners' Association in the following year. He explained that the overproduction of cotton goods in America raised a basic and unavoidable question. "Shall we enter upon a destructive competition between ourselves for the limited business that the home market furnishes," he asked, "or shall we work together to create new trade for the whole United States in competition with Germany, France, England and other foreign countries?"[5] Along with Tompkins, the members of the association preferred the export option. "Much valuable energy may be expended in a rivalry within a limited market," the *Manufacturers' Record* concurred. "The same energy exerted for the promotion of common interests in a wider market will undoubtedly have a beneficial effect both North and South."[6]

Manufactures (Charlotte, N.C.: published by the author, 1900). See also Tompkins to Senator Benjamin R. Tillman, December 26, 1899; Tompkins to A. R. Smith, December 26, 1899; and Tompkins to Theodore C. Search, February 2, 1900, Tompkins Letterbook, Southern Historical Collection, University of North Carolina Library, Chapel Hill.

[4] *Boston Journal of Commerce*, May 28, 1898, p. 149; also quoted in *Textile World*, June 1898, pp. 31–32.

[5] *Bradstreet's*, June 3, 1899, p. 350; also quoted in *American Trade*, May 15, 1899, p. 121.

[6] *Manufacturers' Record*, May 19, 1899, p. 275.

Tompkins likewise urged the New England Cotton Manufacturers' Association in 1899 to accept his plea for domestic cooperation to advance foreign commerce. "The cotton factories of America now make enough goods in eight months to meet all local demand," Tompkins warned his Yankee audience. "The question with Americans now is what shall be done with the output of the mills for the other four months?" Increased shipments to Asia would allow for continued industrial development, he asserted; but if the China market were lost, the country already had too many spinning and weaving establishments. "The most vital question which concerns the cotton milling industry in the United States," Tompkins concluded, "lies along the line of the country making sure of its export trade." The applause which interrupted his speech upon ten different occasions signaled a growing willingness among northern textile executives to collaborate with their southern competitors.[7]

The New England Cotton Manufacturers' Association gave Tompkins another warm reception a year later. He advocated reciprocal trade treaties to secure overseas outlets for coarse cloth produced in the South and to protect the home market for finer fabrics made in the North. Tompkins then repeated the argument that the existence of domestic overproduction demanded a redefinition of enemies. "The competitions of the world are rather betwixt nation and nation than betwixt individuals of the same nation," he asserted. Hence northern and southern textile leaders should band "together in the war of commerce to get our proportion of the trade of the world in competition with Germany and England and France and any other country that wants to come into competition with us." The address won great applause. "Cooperation," the president of the organization agreed, "will contribute material advantage to the interest of both sections."[8]

Meanwhile, the New South's rapidly growing China trade promised to keep the entire American cotton industry in a healthy condition. Although statistical records revealing the exact percentage of southern output exported to the Far East are unavailable, the existing evidence indicates that it was quite significant. Many large textile establishments owned and operated by southerners

---

[7] *Transactions of the New England Cotton Manufacturers' Association*, October 5, 1899, pp. 96–107.

[8] *Transactions of the New England Cotton Manufacturers' Association*, October 18, 1900, pp. 282–94.

sold almost exclusively to northern China and Manchuria. "There was not a hole in the East," one American reported back, "where I did not find a Piedmont brand."[9] A few New England firms, like the giant Pepperell Manufacturing Company in Maine, did continue to make impressive shipments to Asia. But most cotton fabrics sent to the Orient bearing northern trademarks had been produced by Yankee branch factories located in the South.[10]

Contemporary reports made it clear that the southern cotton industry had become the nation's leading business interest in Asia by the end of the century. Not only did China take over half of all the American cloth shipped overseas, but cotton goods made up more than half of the country's total sales to the Celestial Empire.[11] Between 1887 and 1897, American exports of plain gray and white fabrics to China jumped by 121.11 percent in quantity and 59.4 percent in value, while British exports decreased by 13.77 percent in quantity and 7.9 percent in value.[12] Southern textile manufacturers seemed to be pushing their English rivals out of the Orient, and the great potential of the China market appeared to be materializing just in time to enable the New South to sustain its cotton mill campaign.

But ugly clouds gathering over the Far East soon cast a dark shadow on these delightful prospects. European powers were maneuvering in early 1898 to carve the Chinese Empire into exclusive spheres of influence. Germany received special privileges in the Shantung district, France extended its control in the three southern provinces, and Russia moved into Manchuria. Britain then reluctantly joined the venture by extracting recognition of its economic interests in the Yangtze Valley. The Russian advance particularly disturbed southern textile manufacturers because most of their exports to Asia were destined for northern China, and especially Manchuria. The Russians were already selling coarse fabrics in these areas, and the alarm went out that Russia might interfere with the New South's mushrooming China trade.[13]

---

[9] *Manufacturers' Record*, October 14, 1898.

[10] U.S., Congress, House, Industrial Commission on the Relations and Conditions of Capital and Labor, Report, *House Document* No. 495, 56th Cong., 2nd sess., 1901, p. 516.

[11] U.S., Department of State, *Consular Report* No. 239 (August 1900), pp. 474–75.

[12] *Consular Report* No. 233 (April 1899), p. 560.

[13] *Transactions of the New England Cotton Manufacturers' Association*, October 28, 1897, p. 342.

These fears had been intensified by a recent French assault against American commerce in Madagascar. For some years American manufacturers had dominated the cotton goods trade in that French colony, but the situation changed abruptly in 1897 when France imposed a discriminatory tariff giving its own merchandise a strong preference. The next two years brought a sharp decline in the amount of American cloth imported into Madagascar, while French fabrics made striking gains.[14] Some leading southern entrepreneurs, like Ellison A. Smyth of the huge Pelzer Manufacturing Company, lost a profitable business in Madagascar, and they transferred that experience to the threatening situation in China.[15]

The apprehension grew that Russia would soon implement an exclusionist policy in Manchuria. The *New York Journal of Commerce and Commercial Bulletin* cited the misfortune in Madagascar as a warning that the same thing could happen in China.[16] John Barrett, the former American minister to Siam, likewise regarded the growing Russian influence in northern China as a direct threat to the large importation of southern textile products into that region. "It therefore behooves us," he declared, "to see that there is no discrimination against such imports in favor of the output from the new cotton mills of southern Russia which are preparing to compete for the Asiatic trade."[17]

Southern textile spokesmen expressed acute anxiety about the Russian menace. "Conditions in China are such," the *Manufacturers' Record* exclaimed in 1899, "that a slight turn of the wheel may either block American chances there indefinitely or produce a wonderful expansion of American markets." The editors urged southern leaders "to impress upon public opinion the vital necessity of preventing the wheel being turned in the wrong direction."[18] Tompkins continued to do his part. "With that trade and its future extension secured, we have a vast opportunity for extending the production and manufacture of cotton," he argued. "We may then

---

[14] American imports of cotton goods into Madagascar dropped in value from $431,688 in 1897 down to $245 in 1899, while French imports correspondingly jumped in value from $97,340 up to $1,542,858. These figures are cited in Charles S. Campbell, Jr., *Special Business Interests and the Open Door Policy* (New Haven: Yale University Press, 1951), p. 21.

[15] *Manufacturers' Record*, November 30, 1899, p. 312.

[16] *New York Journal of Commerce and Commercial Bulletin*, January 5, 1898.

[17] *Asia, Journal of the American Asiatic Association*, March 17, 1900, p. 83.

[18] *Manufacturers' Record*, July 7, 1899, p. 395.

build more and more mills to the limit of available labor. If we lose that trade then we have too many mills already. If our government fails to take steps to insure the integrity of the Chinese Empire and protect our trade there under our treaty rights with China, then Russia will make the cotton and cotton goods for the present and future trade in Manchuria where so far most of our trade lies."[19]

The National Association of Manufacturers actively supported its constituents in the New South in their effort to keep the door into China open. Southern textile leaders had helped launch the organization in 1895 to secure aid in their drive to penetrate Latin American markets. As their exports to China augmented, however, the NAM shifted some of its promotional work to the Asian field. President Theodore C. Search explained that "no American industry has so much at stake in the future of the Orient as the manufacture of cotton goods."[20] As the fear of Russian domination in Manchuria heightened in early 1899, Search pointed out that "cotton is one of the subjects that is now especially taking the attention of the association."[21]

The American Asiatic Association also maintained a close watch over the New South's expanding overseas business. The New York and Boston commission houses, which handled the products of several large southern cotton mills, established the organization in early 1898 in order to safeguard their mercantile interests in the Far East. Secretary of the Interior Cornelius N. Bliss, a partner in one of these export firms, provided the AAA with a direct contact in Washington. The Russian menace in Manchuria spurred him and his colleagues to try to influence the McKinley administration "with frequent personal calls and correspondence." The constant pressure did not go unnoticed. "Our suggestions and resolutions," President Everett Frazer noted, "have been received with warm appreciation."[22]

Beyond acting through these business groups, southern cotton manufacturers united with northerners in direct agitation for an Open Door policy. Many mill owners and commission houses peti-

---

[19] Tompkins, *American Commerce, Its Expansion*, pp. 79–80.
[20] *Manufacturers' Record*, May 17, 1900, pp. 279–80.
[21] Industrial Commission, Report, *House Document* No. 495, pp. 125–26.
[22] Campbell, *Special Business Interests and the Open Door Policy*, p. 57. See chap. 4 for an excellent discussion of the founding of the AAA.

tioned Secretary of State John Hay in January 1899 for the protection of their Far Eastern commerce. They informed him that well over half of all American cotton textile exports went to areas in China already occupied or endangered by Russia. "Unless a vigorous policy is pursued on the part of the United States Government," they pleaded, "these markets will be eventually closed to our trade, as has recently been the case in Madagascar. The territory threatened by Russia is much more important to us than to England, as her lighter goods find a larger market in the more Southern parts of China; hence we must look after our own interests in the North of China, and not rely on the assistance which England might give us." They concluded their appeal by asking that the American representatives in Russia and China be instructed to give the matter special consideration.[23]

Secretary of State Hay reacted in a positive manner. He promptly sent copies of the petition to Minister Edwin H. Conger in Peking and Herbert H. D. Pierce, *chargé d'affaires* in St. Petersburg, advising both diplomats that "the high character and standing of the signers" warranted calling "serious attention to the subject." Hay later reminded Pierce that he should use "every opportunity to act energetically in the sense desired by the numerous and influential signers of the petition."[24] Then, in September 1899, Hay dispatched the first set of Open Door Notes, asking the various interested European and Asian powers to join with the United States in a formal declaration supporting the territorial integrity of the Chinese Empire and the principle of equal trade opportunities in each of the provinces.

Several notable South Carolina cotton mill owners almost immediately addressed letters to their congressmen exhorting them to make sure that the government would remain committed to the Open Door policy. "The business of cotton manufacturing is the paramount manufacturing interest of the State," they explained. "Next to agriculture, it is the principal employment of our people. It returns wages directly to a very large percentage of our population, and indirectly it is the support of many thousands more. A large number of mills in this State are making goods for the China or Eastern trade. If by any chance this demand should be cut off, the mills would be compelled to shut down, or get into direct

---

[23] Record Group 59, Department of State, Miscellaneous Letters, January 3, 1899, National Archives, Washington, D.C.

[24] Campbell, *Special Business Interests and the Open Door Policy*, pp. 47–48.

competition with other mills which are making goods for home consumption. You can at once see what the importance of the China trade is to us; it is everything." The factory managers believed that the economic health of South Carolina depended upon their commerce in China. "Given the open door," they concluded, "we have no fears as to result or as to the future prosperity of our Commonwealth."[25]

Textile interests in other southern states likewise stood firmly behind the Open Door policy. The *Southern and Western Textile Excelsior* reported in November 1899 that "a majority of cotton mill men of the South are heartily in favor of keeping our markets in the Orient open and of pursuing such a course of action as will most benefit trade in these markets."[26] *Dixie* agreed with the cotton manufacturers that "no section of the country will derive more immediate and material benefit from a vigorous foreign policy than the South."[27] A year later, former Senator John B. Gordon of Georgia succinctly stated the basic strategy demanded by the expansionist consensus in the southern states. "We want the open door," he cried, "and a big one at that."[28]

Spokesmen for the New England cotton industry also backed the Open Door policy. The *Textile World* expressed the general sentiment in forceful language. "Our commerce with China and the countries of Eastern Asia," the editors declared, "depends for its development upon what is now known as 'the open door' policy."[29] This outlook prompted northerners to combine with southerners in a movement to establish a commercial commission to investigate market conditions in the Orient. Representative William C. Lovering of Massachusetts, who had earlier proposed legislation intended to throttle industrial growth in the cotton states, explained his support for the project in terms of a desire to help southern textile manufacturers enlarge their Far Eastern trade.[30]

---

[25] See, for the full text of the letter, U.S., Congress, Senate, *Congressional Record*, 56th Cong., 1st sess., February 28, 1900, 33, pt. 3: 2384–85; *Manufacturers' Record*, October 20, 1899, p. 212; or *Textile World*, November 1899, pp. 36–37.

[26] *Southern and Western Textile Excelsior*, November 11, 1899, p. 10.

[27] *Dixie*, November 1899, p. 23.

[28] *Chattanooga Tradesman*, December 15, 1900, p. 53.

[29] *Textile World*, February 1900, p. 225. See also December 1899, p. 29; September 1898, pp. 25–26.

[30] U.S., Congress, House, *Congressional Record*, 56th Cong., 1st sess., April 30, 1900, 33, pt. 6: 4877.

An editorial in the *Boston Journal of Commerce* spelled out the basis for New England's decision to enter into an alliance with the New South. "The present outlook is that it will be many years before we will again be burdened with an overproduction," the editors noted in 1899, "but such a time is sure to come, and will again place us in the throes of another business depression unless we prepare an outlet for the surplus." Consequently, the editors concluded, "it is not only for the interest of southern cotton mills, but also for our northern ones, that their congressional representatives, irrespective of party politics, should work together and do their utmost to see that this government takes a firm stand and see that China and all other eastern countries are governed by the Open Door' policy."[31]

Meanwhile, the United States had declared war against Spain in April 1898 after the Madrid government demonstrated its inability to pacify the Cuban revolution. Even before hostilities in the Caribbean commenced, Admiral George Dewey set sail across the Pacific to destroy the Spanish fleet stationed in the Philippine Islands. Dewey's smashing victory in Manila Bay left America with the opportunity of acquiring a coaling, cable, and naval base in the Far East. The chief issue in the ensuing debate over the tactics of imperialism was soon clarified. Did the country need a stronghold in the Philippines to be able to insist upon adherence to the Open Door policy in China?

The cotton mill owners of the New South quickly jumped into the controversy over the merits of engaging in a limited amount of territorial expansion in order to gain a large noncolonial market. Their answers to a questionnaire sent out by the *Manufacturers' Record* in June 1898 demonstrated their early and eager desire to exploit the spoils of the war with Spain. Several prominent southern textile leaders, such as James L. Orr, H. H. Hickman, Ellison A. Smyth, and Daniel A. Tompkins, responded by favoring the retention of the Philippine Islands. Some did register opposition, and still others had not yet made up their minds. Even with his uncertainty, John F. Hanson was particularly candid. "It is a cold question of business," he commented, "and I am in favor of or opposed to annexation according to the measure of advantage or disadvantage that will come to us from one or the other course."[32]

---

[31] *Boston Journal of Commerce*, November 4, 1899, p. 110. See also June 2, 1900, p. 194.

[32] *Manufacturers' Record*, June 17, 1898, pp. 339–41. See also June 24, 1898, p. 355.

Southern cotton manufacturers increasingly concluded that America should exercise sufficient control over the Philippines to keep the door into China open. The swing in this direction was expedited by influential industrialists who appealed to American history to quiet uneasiness about the possible ill effects of territorial aggrandizement. Smyth pointed out that landed "expansion has been the policy of this country since the days of George Washington."[33] Tompkins similarly noted that "we have had colonies in this country ever since we ceased to be colonies ourselves."[34] Arguments by outside opinion makers, like John Barrett, also had the intended results. Tompkins privately complimented Barrett in October 1899 after one of his southern lectures. "Quite a number of important cotton manufacturers have said to me that heretofore they have been on the anti-expansion side of the Philippine question," Tompkins wrote, "but after hearing your speech they are entirely convinced of the former error and now favor expansion."[35]

Southern business journals agreed that the country needed a power base in the Far East. The *Southern and Western Textile Excelsior*, for example, believed that the possession of the Philippine Islands would enable America to demand equal commercial opportunity on the Chinese mainland. "Is the present development of the export trade in the South to be overdrawn and all possibilities of future progress in this line to be foregone because of a wild cry of imperialism in some quarters?" asked the editors. "No, imperialism is a bugaboo."[36] The same reasoning led the *Manufacturers' Record* to denounce those who were "endeavoring to prevent the United States from enjoying the perfectly legitimate fruits of Dewey's victory in Manila Bay."[37]

Senator John L. McLaurin of South Carolina assumed a position of leadership in the drive for insular imperialism. He made a strong argument in October 1899 that the United States needed to retain the Philippine Islands in order to enforce the Open Door policy in China. "My judgment is that the control of them, or at least of some portions," he asserted, "is the only safeguard for our trade interests in the East. The abandonment of them means the dismemberment of China, its partition among the European pow-

---

[33] *Manufacturers' Record*, November 30, 1899, pp. 312–16.

[34] Tompkins, *American Commerce, Its Expansion*, p. 21.

[35] Daniel A. Tompkins to John Barrett, October 31, 1899, Tompkins Letterbook.

[36] *Southern and Western Textile Excelsior*, October 21, 1899, p. 10.

[37] *Manufacturers' Record*, October 20, 1899, p. 212.

ers, and the inevitable loss of our China trade." He observed that the issue was "fraught with momentous consequences" for the textile business in his section of the country because the China market was "the hope of this great manufacturing industry in the South."[38]

Senator McLaurin, however, confronted a difficult situation in South Carolina. He wanted desperately to help the cotton manufacturers protect their China trade. But fellow Senator Benjamin R. Tillman opposed the acquisition of the Philippines, and as a leading Democrat in the state he made every effort to keep McLaurin in line. Despite fears that he would suffer politically, McLaurin still decided to come out openly for annexation in order to aid the mill owners.[39] He told the members of the American Asiatic Association in early 1900 that he would not be deterred by "the specter of imperialism" sprung by his enemies for political reasons. "I will vote for the retention of these islands," he cried. "If this be imperialism, let them make the most of it."[40]

Many other southern politicians, though strong supporters of overseas economic expansion, remained tied to the Democratic opposition to maritime acquisitions. Senator Augustus O. Bacon of Georgia, for example, believed the Open Door policy would greatly benefit the South; yet he presented many arguments against even a small amount of colonialism. "To come down to the practical point," Bacon emphasized in 1900, "we do not need any help in the Philippine Islands to get into China."[41] Congressman Stanyarne Wilson of South Carolina likewise dismissed the argument that the Philippines provided the key to the door into China. "What we need is not possession of these islands of the sea," Wilson insisted, "but an open door to Asia. That is important—immensely important—to us. Force or vast colonial possessions are not useful or necessary to open that door."[42]

These politicians of the New South, like the cotton manufactur-

---

[38] Ibid.

[39] Richard H. Davis, Jr., "The Role of South Carolina's Cotton Manufacturing in the United States' Far Eastern Policy," (M.A. thesis, University of South Carolina, 1966), pp. 21–32.

[40] *Manufacturers' Record*, February 1, 1900, pp. 20–21.

[41] U.S., Congress, Senate, *Congressional Record*, 56th Cong., 1st sess., January 30, 1900, 33, pt. 2: 1309.

[42] U.S., Congress, House, *Congressional Record*, 56th Cong., 1st sess., February 22, 1900, 33, pt. 3: 2104.

ers they represented, assumed that the China market was vitally important to the prosperity of their section. Some wanted to impose formal control over the Philippines so that the United States could enforce its will in China. Most disapproved. But the crucial point is that the southerners centered their debate on the issue of how to attain foreign markets. They did not ask the more basic question of whether a fundamental change in the capitalist system would provide a viable alternative to their export commitment. Even those southerners who opposed the colonization of the Philippines favored the establishment of an informal empire in China.

At the same time, the congressional dispute over the Philippine question revealed the collaboration among northern and southern cotton mill interests in support of the Open Door policy. Henry Cabot Lodge, for example, concurred with McLaurin that America should retain the islands to prevent Russia from destroying its rapidly growing cotton goods trade in China. "Nearly all these cotton manufactures," Lodge explained in 1900, "came from the South, and have been to our Southern mills a source of great profit, while at the same time they have relieved the pressure upon the domestic market and are thus a direct benefit to every cotton factory in New England."[43] The agreement between the senator from Massachusetts and the senator from South Carolina symbolized the relationship between the politics of reunion and the policy of expansion. Lodge had given up his bill to force the South to let blacks vote, and southerners like McLaurin were turning away from the race issue and concentrating their attention on economic matters.[44]

The Southern Cotton Spinners' Association unanimously adopted a series of resolutions in November 1899 that nicely illustrate the inclusive and interrelated nature of the expansionist program. The organization, which represented textile leaders from every part of the South, addressed these recommendations to the president and Congress. The group urged the construction of an isthmian canal, the laying of a cable across the Pacific, and the suppression of the revolution in the Philippines as part of a design

---

[43] U.S., Congress, Senate, *Congressional Record*, 56th Cong., 1st sess., March 7, 1900, 33, pt. 3: 2629.

[44] See, for example, Henry Cabot Lodge to B. F. Ruley, November 19, 1894, Lodge Letterbook, Massachusetts Historical Society, Boston; and Daniel A. Tompkins to Richard H. Edmonds, July 10, 1900, Tompkins Papers, Library of Congress, Washington, D.C.

to preserve the integrity of the Chinese Empire and to maintain an open door into that country. The association further advised working with England and Japan if necessary to defend treaty rights guaranteeing unrestricted trade in China and "such increases in our navy as will make it fully adequate to protect our commerce in all seas and in all parts of the world."[45]

The annual meeting of the Southern Cotton Spinners' Association a year later dramatized the maturation of the imperial consensus. President J. H. McAden set the tone by calling for the retention of the Philippines and the maintenance of the Open Door in China. Then Tompkins advocated sectional cooperation in securing the means necessary for the enlargement of American commerce. He asserted that "democrats and republicans alike ought to demand of and support our government in a vigorous prosecution of all measures looking to the protection and extension of our interests in what was once the old far East, and what is now our new far West." A set of resolutions, introduced by Tompkins and adopted unanimously, committed the association to pressure Congress for financial assistance in providing the facilities required for exploiting the new frontier.[46]

The complete accord regarding the dominant theme of the meeting deeply impressed the editor of the *Manufacturers' Record*. "Over and over again in the speeches that were made," Richard H. Edmonds reported, "the warning was given to politicians that the time had come when the businessmen of the South proposed to unite with the businessmen of the North in demanding legislation that would be in the best interest of the country without regard to what the politicians of either party might prefer." Edmonds was moved by "the enthusiasm with which every speech advocating subsidies to American steamship lines, the building of the Nicaraguan canal and the maintenance of the open door in China and the retention of the Philippine Islands was received." Maintaining close rapport with the delegates during the meetings and over bourbon, he "failed to hear one single word of dissent from the propositions stated." Edmonds concluded that the prevailing spirit of economic nationalism indicated "a revolution in Southern sentiment."[47]

---

[45] *Asia, Journal of the American Asiatic Association*, November 13, 1899, p. 68.
[46] *Manufacturers' Record*, May 17, 1900, pp. 277–83.
[47] *Manufacturers' Record*, June 21, 1900, pp. 364–65.

A cotton mill boom in the New South, in the meantime, made the uncertain situation in Asia appear all the more serious. Informed sources, like Ellison A. Smyth of the Pelzer Company, pointed out that the decision to construct many of the rising textile enterprises in the southern states had been based upon the assumption of a brisk business in China. "Most of these new mills are being built for the export trade, and particularly the trade with the East," Smyth explained in 1899, "and the money that is being invested there is in jeopardy if our export trade is not maintained and fostered." He foresaw untold harm for southern cotton manufacturing if "the doors of China closed against us."[48]

The outbreak of the Boxer Rebellion in the spring of 1900 verified his prediction. The anti-foreign riots, which centered in northern China, disrupted the cotton goods trade in that area and depressed the southern textile industry.[49] As American cloth exports to China dropped in value from $10,278,487 in 1899 down to $5,205,892 in 1900, plans for the erection of new factories in the South were shelved.[50] The disturbance also hurt some New England firms, like the Pepperell Company, and other northern manufacturers feared that they would suffer indirectly from the southern losses.[51] Strictures that cotton mill masters should have avoided such a disaster by cultivating other foreign markets only underscored the importance of the Oriental trade.[52] The immediate situation was painful, but the long-range dangers seemed even worse.

The Boxer Rebellion provoked intense anxiety that European countries would use the uprising as an excuse for violating the Open Door promises of the previous fall and partitioning China into spheres of influence. The *Boston Journal of Commerce* warned that if either Germany or Russia had its way in China, "it would

---

[48] *Manufacturers' Record*, November 30, 1899, pp. 312–13.

[49] *Boston Journal of Commerce*, July 14, 1900, p. 314; *Chattanooga Tradesman*, August 1, 1900, p. 79; and *Dixie*, August 1900, p. 40.

[50] John H. Montgomery and his associates provide a good illustration of the way southern cotton mill building fluctuated with events in Asia. They postponed construction of their Gainesville factory when the effects of the Boxer Rebellion hit, but they decided to complete the enterprise after the China trade resumed. See Allen Stokes, "John H. Montgomery: Pioneer Southern Industrialist" (M.A. thesis, University of South Carolina, 1967), chap. 6.

[51] *Dixie*, August 1900, p. 35; and *American Trade*, August 1, 1900, p. 156.

[52] *Boston Journal of Commerce*, July 21, 1900, p. 334; and August 18, 1900, p. 414.

mean that the vast outlet for the production of our Southern cotton mills would be closed forever, and such a state of affairs would not look well for the future of our cotton industry."[53] Southern newspapers and business periodicals likewise fretted about the possibility of permanently losing their China trade. "The Southern people have a peculiar interest in the solution of the Chinese question," the *Macon News* exclaimed. "They do not want the great country with its teeming millions to be divided among the European powers."[54]

Spokesmen for the New South had come to define the China market as essential to their present prosperity and future welfare, and many were willing to employ force to accomplish their imperial objectives. "We believe it is the duty of all good citizens of the United States to support the present administration in its efforts to protect our treaty rights in China," the *Richmond Times* declared, "and if they have to send troops from Manila or from San Francisco to do so, it should be done."[55] Southern cotton manufacturers were equally militant in their pleas for vigorous action to counter the new threat to the Open Door in the Far East. Several of them signed a memorial the American Asiatic Association sent to President William McKinley in June 1900 urging him to act energetically to restore order in China.[56]

The McKinley administration responded favorably to the strong demands made by the southern textile leaders and their New England allies. Other special business interests, such as the kerosene and flour exporters, added their voices to the mounting expansionist chorus. These narrowly conceived appeals reinforced the broader outlook shared by elite groups that the successful functioning of the entire American economic system depended upon foreign markets.[57] Such considerations prompted high echelon policy makers to react to the Boxer Rebellion by dispatching in

---

[53] *Boston Journal of Commerce*, June 16, 1900, p. 234. See also June 30, 1900, p. 274.

[54] *Macon News*, as quoted in *Dixie*, July 1900, p. 40. See also *Southern and Western Textile Excelsior*, June 16, 1900, p. 10.

[55] *Richmond Times*, as quoted in *Dixie*, July 1900, pp. 40–41.

[56] *Manufacturers' Record*, June 28, 1900, p. 381.

[57] William A. Williams, *The Tragedy of American Diplomacy* (New York: Dell Publishing Co., 1962); Walter LaFeber, *The New Empire: An Interpretation of American Expansion, 1860–1898* (Ithaca: Cornell University Press, 1963); and Thomas J. McCormick, *China Market: America's Quest for Informal Empire, 1893–1901* (Chicago: Quadrangle Press, 1967).

July 1900 a second set of Open Door Notes. A month later, they ordered American troops on duty in the Philippines to join an international army to help suppress the insurrection in China, thereby strengthening the hand of the United States against its European and Asian rivals.

The lords of the loom in the New South were grateful for the administration's forceful conduct in their behalf, and in November 1900 several of them formalized their feelings in the following memorial addressed to Secretary of State Hay: "The undersigned manufacturers of cotton goods in the Southern States desire to express their approval of the action of the United States Government in the protection of American interests in China, known as the 'open door' policy, and trust this position may be maintained, and more especially relating to Manchuria, to which section of the Chinese Empire a large proportion of the production of the cotton drills and sheetings manufactured in the Southern States is exported."[58] The man responsible for circulating the petition noted that not a single firm to which it was presented refused to sign it.[59]

The southerners also continued to combine with northerners in exerting pressure on the government to protect their interests in the Far East. Many southern mill owners endorsed an American Asiatic Association memorial advocating persistent efforts to prevent discriminatory taxation on goods imported into China. Daniel A. Tompkins traveled to Washington with the executive committee in January 1901 to present the petition to the president. The association's official journal reported that "Tompkins made a clear and forcible statement of the position of the cotton manufacturers of the South in regard to the policy of the Administration in China, and pointed out the vital importance to them of a speedy and satisfactory settlement of existing difficulties."[60]

The battle in behalf of the Open Door policy climaxed the movement for cooperation between the two antagonistic regions. Southerners had not abandoned their struggle to achieve economic independence, and they were still bitter about continued Yankee attempts to hinder their industrial development. But their

---

[58] Record Group 46, Records of the United States Senate, 56A-J12.6, National Archives, Washington, D.C.

[59] *Manufacturers' Record*, November 15, 1900, pp. 269–70. The petition was reprinted in *Chattanooga Tradesman*, December 1, 1900, p. 82.

[60] *Asia, Journal of the American Asiatic Association*, January 21, 1901, pp. 118–21.

long involvement in overseas commerce, originally intended to enable them to break the chains of a colonial economy, ironically led them to collaborate with their old New England foes. The almost universal belief that foreign markets were necessary to avoid the ills of domestic overproduction and to allow for sustained cotton mill construction resulted in an alliance between northerners and southerners aimed at solving internal problems through expansion abroad. Thus the sectional reunion at the turn of the century helped lay the foundations for the establishment of America's informal empire.

Courtesy of Pelzer Plants, Pelzer, South Carolina.

Southward the course of industrial supremacy and commercial empire will take its way.

Congressman James Norton of South Carolina, 1900

9

The New South in the Twentieth Century

The New South's quest for economic independence and commercial empire continued on into the twentieth century. Southerners never abandoned hope that the cotton mill campaign would stimulate general industrial development and thereby enable their section to become free from northern economic domination. Southerners also persisted in the belief that their ability to compete successfully in foreign markets would underwrite their drive for wealth and power. These dual themes—independence and empire—remained closely intertwined in southern thinking. Hence the New South continued to engage in commercial expansion abroad in an attempt to break the chains of a colonial economy at home.

At the turn of the century, southerners confidently based their visions of future progress and prosperity upon the assumption of a constantly increasing export trade. "The South for two decades has had a wonderful expansion, industrially and commercially, but it is only the beginning," a southern business journal declared. "The twentieth century, with its isthmian canal and its fleets of merchant ships, will bring to the South the opportunity for development which it needs."[1] A Mississippi mill owner was equally optimistic about the destiny of his section. "With the opening of the Nicaragua canal and the securing of the trade of the Orient by an open-door policy," he proclaimed, "a new era will be opened for the material development of the cotton industry of the South on a

---

[1] *Chattanooga Tradesman*, January 1, 1899, pp. 140–41.

scale never before known in the commercial world."[2] A South Carolina congressman expressed the widespread enthusiasm in a succinct prophecy about the years ahead: "Southward the course of industrial supremacy and commercial empire will take its way."[3]

These sanguine prospects appeared to be materializing during the first two decades of the new century. The American cotton textile industry experienced a period of swift growth and sustained prosperity between 1900 and 1920. Factory managers enlarged their facilities, erected new plants, and enjoyed handsome profits. During these years, American cotton goods held sway in the buoyant domestic market. Synthetic fabrics like rayon had yet to make serious inroads in the trade, and imported dry goods remained noncompetitive with the great bulk of coarse and medium quality cloth produced at home. At the same time, American textile executives gradually expanded their overseas commerce. These years were, as one historian termed them, a "golden age" for cotton manufacturing in the United States.[4]

During this period, the New South continued to challenge New England for dominion in the mushrooming textile industry. Southerners captured an increasingly large share of the business, and by 1920 the former Confederate states possessed almost half of the active cotton spindles in the country. The aggressive southern entrepreneurs were not satisfied with their striking victories in the coarse goods field, and they embarked upon a successful campaign to defeat their northern foes in the production of higher grades of cloth. The results were impressive. The South spun over half of the country's medium yarn by 1914 and more than a quarter of the fine yarn by 1920. These accomplishments encouraged southerners to prepare themselves for the final struggle for national supremacy in the cotton mill business.[5]

The New South's industrial crusade maintained its momentum even during the severe textile depression in the 1920s. Although mill dividends dropped considerably, southerners continued to earn moderate returns on their investments in cotton manufactur-

---

[2] *Manufacturers' Record*, May 24, 1900, p. 229.

[3] U.S., Congress, House, *Congressional Record*, 56th Cong., 1st sess., April 23, 1900, 33, pt. 5: 4570.

[4] Jack Blicksilver, *Cotton Manufacturing in the Southeast: An Historical Analysis* (Atlanta: Bureau of Business and Economic Research, Georgia State College of Business Administration, Bulletin No. 5, July 1959), p. 50.

[5] Ibid., pp. 51–57.

ing. An air of confidence prevailed in Dixie. Southerners built new cotton factories, added equipment to already established workshops, and employed an increasing number of operatives. These significant gains in the southern states, moreover, were made while the nation's overall cotton spindle capacity slowly declined. As a result, by the end of the decade, the South had assumed a commanding position in the production of medium fabrics and had attained control of about two-thirds of the active spindles in the United States.[6]

The New England branch of the cotton textile industry, in the meantime, entered a period of rapid deterioration. The northern manufacturers were burdened with more expensive power, steeper tax rates, older machinery, and higher labor costs compared to their southern opponents. Intensified competition during the depression decade brought great destruction to New England and left that section in second place in the contest for leadership in the textile business. Between 1921 and 1929, about two and a half million cotton spindles were scrapped, and fifty-one northern factories containing more than one and a third million spindles were moved to southern locations. As these losses mounted, a contemporary writer noted that "the columns of the textile press reporting the discontinuance and liquidation and abandonment of New England mills read like wartime casualty lists."[7]

Nevertheless, the New England cotton manufacturers refused to surrender their position without a vigorous fight. During the Progressive era, northern businessmen backed proposals for national labor reforms in order to retard industrial growth in the South. They succeeded, despite strong opposition from the southeastern textile states, in getting a child labor law enacted in 1916, but the Supreme Court soon ruled against it.[8] Chief Justice William H. Taft later explained that the Constitution could not be strained to meet the wishes of "yankee competitors."[9] Yet the New Englanders persisted in their efforts to undermine their adversary's key advantage, and they received some comfort in 1933 when the National Industrial Recovery Act narrowed the labor

---

[6] Ibid., pp. 89–93.

[7] Ibid.

[8] George B. Tindall, *The Emergence of the New South, 1913–1945* (Baton Rouge: Louisiana State University Press, 1967), pp. 16–17, 321–22.

[9] Stanley I. Kutler, "Chief Justice Taft, National Regulation, and the Commerce Power," *Journal of American History* 51 (March 1965): 652.

cost disparity between the two sections. Southern manufacturers complained that the code scales would hamper their economic development, and they applauded two years later when the Court knocked the measure down.[10]

The enduring battle over railroad freight rate discrimination also dramatized the relationship between national reform and the sectional conflict. Southern "progressives" encountered stiff opposition from northern textile interests when they demanded the elimination of these "artificial" barriers to their industrial expansion.[11] During the depression years between the two world wars, the New England manufacturers increased their attempts to secure favorable transportation charges in order to survive the onslaught from Dixie.[12] Southerners responded with an energetic attack against railway discriminations that assumed the character of a sectional crusade. The Southern Governors' Conference spearheaded this movement to destroy the shackles of internal imperialism. The rising agitation finally led the Interstate Commerce Commission in 1945 to pronounce sectional freight rate differentials illegal.[13]

After countering northern maneuvers to stifle their mill building program, southerners entered the post–World War II era prepared to complete their economic conquest over their former military masters. The war provided temporary relief in New England; but the return of peace brought the resumption of liquidations, and within a decade the northern branch of the textile industry suffered virtual annihilation. New England cotton factories, for example, operated only 1.5 million spindles in 1957 compared to 18.1 million active in the South. During the same time, southerners not only achieved dominance in the production of fine cloth, but they also extended their control over the bleaching, dyeing, and finishing end of the business. In short, by the mid-1950s, the New South reigned supreme in cotton manufacturing, while New England stood in humiliation and defeat.[14]

---

[10] Tindall, *The Emergence of the New South*, pp. 433–46.

[11] C. Vann Woodward, *Origins of the New South, 1877–1913* (Baton Rouge: Louisiana State University Press, 1951), pp. 369–95; and Richard M. Abrams, "A Paradox of Progressivism: Massachusetts on the Eve of Insurgency," *Political Science Quarterly* 75 (September 1960): 379–99.

[12] David M. Potter, "The Historical Development of Eastern-Southern Freight Rate Relationships," *Law and Contemporary Problems* 14 (1947): 416–48.

[13] Tindall, *The Emergence of the New South*, pp. 599–603.

[14] Blicksilver, *Cotton Manufacturing in the Southeast*, pp. 147–48.

Triumphant at home, the New South aspired to win even more glorious victories abroad. Southern cotton manufacturers had gradually expanded their overseas trade during the first twenty years of the century, and the textile depression in the next two decades reinforced their traditional export orientation. As usual during periods of dragging domestic demand, mill owners considered the option of curtailing production. But the Cotton Textile Institute, established in 1926 to serve as the trade association for the industry, labored in vain to secure voluntary agreements to limit output. The cotton textile code imposed by the National Industrial Recovery Act in 1933 similarly failed to reduce production sufficiently so that it would not exceed home demand. Southerners therefore looked to foreign commerce to help solve the problem of domestic overproduction.[15]

Unfortunately for the South, however, Japan had already begun its own drive for industrial development and commercial empire. The Yellow Yankees rapidly expanded their textile operations, and their share of the cotton goods trade of the world leaped from only 2 percent in 1912 up to 41 percent by 1933. Armed with a large supply of cheap labor, the Japanese manufacturers severely damaged southern business in China and other foreign markets. Worse yet, the ambitious Japanese also began to ship coarse cotton goods directly into the United States. President Franklin D. Roosevelt responded to the Japanese invasion of the American market in 1936 by ordering a hike in the tariff on yarn and cloth. When this proved inadequate, the harassed mill owners sent a commission to Japan to negotiate an agreement limiting textile exports to the United States.[16]

The Second World War brought renewed confidence to the South. Domestic demand skyrocketed, and Japanese textile imports were terminated after Pearl Harbor. Southerners looked forward to a revived export trade in the postwar years as predictions abounded that it would be a long time before the destroyed Japanese cotton industry could fully recover. Yet, to the surprise of many, Japan doubled its spindle capacity between 1946 and 1951 by installing the most modern equipment. As a result, southern textile exports declined again, and Japanese imports into the United States steadily increased. The besieged southern mill own-

---

[15] Tindall, *The Emergence of the New South*, pp. 362, 436; and Blicksilver, *Cotton Manufacturing in the Southeast*, pp. 119–20, 130–31.

[16] Blicksilver, *Cotton Manufacturing in the Southeast*, pp. 113–17.

ers pressured Japan in 1956 to accept a system of voluntary restrictions on shipments of cotton goods to America. When this failed to stem the tide, southerners turned to the federal government for protection from the Japanese economic menace.[17]

The New South's cotton mill campaign had come full circle. Back at the turn of the century, southern textile leaders talked optimistically about conquering the markets of the world while they ridiculed their northern rivals for demanding tariff protection. A few had warned about future competition from underdeveloped countries, and some had even suggested prohibiting the export of textile machinery to the Orient.[18] But most spokesmen for the cotton industry remained unconcerned about peoples they considered racially or culturally inferior to themselves. Within fifty years, however, the rising cotton factories in Japan presented a serious threat to the South. To add to the irony, southerners reacted in the same way New Englanders, faced earlier with a similar situation, had done. Indeed, their cry for protection from Japanese competition dramatized the fact that southerners had become much like the Yankees they so detested.

Even in the middle of the twentieth century, however, the New South remained in many ways quite different from the metropolitan North. Although the cotton factories had come to the cotton fields, many other industries had stayed behind. And the mills that did migrate to the southern states were often branches of northern firms seeking to exploit the raw materials and cheap labor in the backward region. While such outside investment in the capital scarce South did provide employment for local workers, it also took huge profits out of the section. Hence, a hundred years after the Civil War, the builders of the New South still found themselves in a semi-colonial position inside the modern American Empire.

---

[17] Ibid., pp. 160–62.

[18] Chester Griswold to C. P. Baker, February 12, 1897, Lawrence Manufacturing Company Papers, Miscellaneous Letters, Baker Library, Harvard Business School, Boston.

Bibliography

Archival Sources

National Archives of the United States. Washington, D.C.
   Record Group 43. Records of the United States Participation in International Conferences, Commissions, and Expositions.
   Record Group 46. Records of the United States Senate.
   Record Group 59. Records of the United States Department of State.
   Record Group 233. Records of the United States House of Representatives.

Manuscript Sources

Alabama State Department of Archives and History. Montgomery.
   John T. Morgan Papers.
   Joseph Wheeler Papers.
Clemson University Library, Special Collections. Clemson, S.C.
   Benjamin R. Tillman Papers.
Harvard Business School, Baker Library. Boston.
   Dwight Manufacturing Company Papers.
   Lawrence Manufacturing Company Papers.
Library of Congress. Washington, D.C.
   Samuel Gompers Papers.
   William Gregg Papers.
   John T. Morgan Papers.
   Daniel A. Tompkins Papers.
Massachusetts Historical Society. Boston.
   Edward Atkinson Papers.
   T. Jefferson Coolidge Papers.
   Amos A. Lawrence Papers.
   Henry Cabot Lodge Papers.

Mississippi State Department of Archives and History. Jackson.
James Z. George Papers.
Mississippi State Grange Papers.
Lucius Q. C. Lamar Papers.
University of North Carolina Library, Southern Historical Collection.
Chapel Hill.
Marion Butler Papers.
John F. A. Claiborne Papers.
Daniel A. Tompkins Papers.
Benjamin C. Yancey Papers.

Theses and Dissertations

Beechert, Edward A. "Industrialism in the Southeast, 1870–1914."
Ph.D. dissertation, University of California, Berkeley, 1957.
Chen, Chen-Han. "The Location of the Cotton Manufacturing Industry
in the United States, 1880–1910." Ph.D. dissertation, Harvard University, 1939.
Clay, Howard B. "Daniel Augustus Tompkins: An American Bourbon."
Ph.D. dissertation, University of North Carolina, 1950.
Davis, Richard H. "The Role of South Carolina's Cotton Manufacturers
in the United States' Far Eastern Policy." M.A. thesis, University of
South Carolina, 1966.
Ferguson, James S. "Agrarianism in Mississippi, 1871–1900: A Study in
Nonconformity." Ph.D. dissertation, University of North Carolina,
1952.
Ide, Yoshmitsu. "The Significance of Richard Hathaway Edmonds and
His *Manufacturers' Record* in the New South." Ph.D. dissertation,
University of Florida, 1959.
Mendenhall, Marjorie S. "A History of Agriculture in South Carolina,
1790 to 1860: An Economic and Social Study." Ph.D. dissertation,
University of North Carolina, 1940.
Pierpont, Andrew W. "Development of the Textile Industry in Alamance
County, North Carolina." Ph.D. dissertation, University of North
Carolina, 1953.
Stokes, Allen. "John H. Montgomery, Pioneer Southern Industrialist."
M.A. thesis, University of South Carolina, 1967.
Terrill, Tom E. "The United States and the Congo, 1883–1885: The Second Liberia." M.A. thesis, University of Wisconsin, 1963.
Webber, Carl L. *"De Bow's Review* and the Movement for Southern Economic Independence, 1846–1861." M.S. thesis, University of Wisconsin, 1949.
Williamson, Gustavus G. "Cotton Manufacturers in South Carolina,
1865–1892." Ph.D. dissertation, Johns Hopkins University, 1954.

Government Publications

U.S., Congress, *Congressional Globe.* 1865–1873.

U.S., Congress, *Congressional Record.* 1873–1900.

U.S., Congress, *House Documents.* 1865–1900.

U.S., Congress, *Senate Documents.* 1865–1900.

U.S., Department of Commerce and Labor, *Statistical Abstract of the United States.* 1910.

U.S., Department of Interior, *Tenth Census of the United States.* 1880, Manufactures, 8, pt. 2.

U.S., Department of Interior, *Twelfth Census of the United States.* 1900, Manufactures, 9, pt. 3.

U.S., Department of State, *Consular Reports.* 1881–1900.

U.S., Treasury Department, Bureau of Statistics, *Monthly Summary of Imports and Exports of the United States.* N.s., 1, 1893–1894.

Pamphlets and Proceedings

Address of Edward Atkinson of Boston, Massachusetts, Given in Atlanta, Georgia, in October, 1880 for the Promotion of an International Cotton Exposition. Boston: A. Williams and Co., 1881.

Baucher, Chauncey S. *The Antebellum Attitudes of South Carolina towards Manufacturing and Agriculture.* St. Louis: Washington University Studies, series 4, vol. 3, pt. 2, April 1916.

Hargrove, H. H. *Louisiana and Mississippi's Prosperity to Be Sought in Cotton Mills: How Cotton Manufacturing Can Be Made to Pay in Small Country Towns and Enrich the Cotton Grower.* New Orleans: Picayune, 1899.

Massachusetts General Court, Senate, *Report of the Committee on Labor No. 270.* Boston: n.p., May 18, 1898.

Official Guide to the Cotton States and International Exposition Held at Atlanta, Ga., Sept. 18 to Dec. 31, 1895. Atlanta: n.p., June 19, 1895.

Proceedings and Transactions of the New England Cotton Manufacturers' Association, 1866–1900.

Proceedings and Transactions of the South Carolina Agricultural and Mechanical Society, 1869–1891.

Agricultural Journals

Carolina Farmer. Wilmington, N.C., 1869–1871.

National Economist. Washington, D.C., 1889–1893.

Plantation. Atlanta, Ga., 1870–1873.

Planters' Journal. Vicksburg, Miss., 1881–1887.
Progressive Farmer. Raleigh, N.C., 1886–1892.
Reconstructed Farmer. Tarboro, N.C., 1869–1872.
Rural Alabamian. Mobile, Ala., 1872–1873.
Rural Carolinian. Charleston, S.C., 1869–1876.
Rural Southerner. Atlanta, Ga., 1870–1874.
Southern Farm and Home. Macon, Ga., 1869–1872.
Southern Field and Factory. Jackson, Miss. 1871–1873.
Southern Plantation. Montgomery, Ala., 1874–1878.
State Agricultural Journal. Raleigh, N.C., 1873–1875.

Trade Journals

American Trade. New York, 1897–1900.
Asia, Journal of the American Asiatic Association. New York, 1898–1900.
Boston Commercial Bulletin. Massachusetts, 1867–1868.
Boston Journal of Commerce. Massachusetts, 1882–1900.
Bradstreet's. New York, 1879–1900.
Bulletin of the American Iron and Steel Association. Philadelphia,
    1880–1886.
Chattanooga Tradesman. Tennessee, 1890–1900.
De Bow's Review. New Orleans, 1846–1879.
Dixie. Atlanta, 1894–1900.
Hunt's Merchants' Magazine. New York, 1839–1870.
Manufacturers' Record. Baltimore, 1883–1900.
New York Commercial and Financial Chronicle. New York, 1865–1900.
Niles' Register. Baltimore, 1827–1832.
South. New York, 1876–1882.
Southern and Western Textile Excelsior. Charlotte, N.C., 1899–1900.
Textile Manufacturers' Review and Industrial Record. New York,
    1887–1894.
Textile Record of America. Philadelphia, 1880–1900.
Textile World. New York, 1897–1900.
Weekly Iron Age. Birmingham, Ala., 1884.

Newspapers

Atlanta Constitution. Georgia, 1880–1882.
Augusta Chronicle and Constitutionalist. Georgia, 1878–1880.
Carolina Spartan. Spartanburg, S.C., 1879–1882.
Charleston Courier. South Carolina, 1866–1867.
Charleston News and Courier. South Carolina, 1879–1882.
Daily Columbus Enquirer. Georgia, 1866.

Greenville Enterprise. South Carolina, 1871–1879.
Huntsville Weekly Democrat. Alabama, 1880–1884.
New Orleans Price-Current. Louisiana, 1865–1870.
Southern Recorder. Milledgeville, Ga., 1865–1870.

Literary Periodicals

Land We Love. Charlotte, N.C., 1866–1869.
XIX Century. Charleston, S.C., 1869–1870.
Scott's Monthly Magazine. Atlanta, Ga., 1865–1869.
Southern Magazine. Baltimore, Md., 1868–1875.

Articles

Abrams, Richard M. "A Paradox of Progressivism, Massachusetts on the Eve of Insurgency." *Political Science Quarterly* 75 (September 1960): 379–99.

Barrett, John. "The Paramount Power in the Pacific." *North American Review* 169 (August 1899): 165–79.

Blicksilver, Jack. "The International Cotton Exposition of 1881 and Its Impact upon the Economic Development of Georgia." *Cotton History Review* 1 (October 1960): 175–94.

Clark, Victor S. "Manufacturing during the Ante-Bellum and War Periods." *The South in the Building of the Nation* 5 (Richmond, Va.: Southern Historical Society, 1909): 313–35.

———. "Modern Manufacturing Development in the South, 1880–1905." *The South in the Building of the Nation* 6 (Richmond, Va.: Southern Historical Society, 1909): 264–304.

Clay, Howard B. "Daniel Augustus Tompkins: The Role of a New South Industrialist in Politics." *Studies in the History of the South* 3 (Greenville, N.C.: East Carolina College Publications in History, 1966): 85–118.

Collins, Herbert. "The Southern Industrial Gospel before 1860." *Journal of Southern History* 12 (August 1946): 386–402.

———. "The Idea of a Cotton Textile Industry in the South, 1870–1900." *North Carolina Historical Review* 34 (July 1957): 358–92.

Davidson, Philip G. "Industrialism in the Ante-Bellum South." *South Atlantic Quarterly* 27 (October 1928): 405–25.

Easterby, J. H. "The Granger Movement in South Carolina." *South Carolina Historical Association Proceedings* 1 (1931): 21–32.

Griffin, Richard W. "Pro-Industrial Sentiment and Cotton Factories in Arkansas, 1820–1863." *Arkansas Historical Quarterly* 15 (Summer 1956): 125–39.

——. "Cotton Manufacturing in Alabama to 1865." *Alabama Historical Quarterly* 18 (Fall 1956): 289–307.

——. "The Augusta (Georgia) Manufacturing Company in Peace, War and Reconstruction, 1847–1877." *Business History Review* 32 (Spring 1958): 60–73.

——. "The Origins of the Industrial Revolution in Georgia: Cotton Textiles, 1810–1865." *Georgia Historical Quarterly* 42 (December 1958): 355–75.

——. "Origins of Southern Cotton Manufactures, 1807–16." *Cotton History Review* 1 (January 1960): 5–12.

——. "The Fisher Committee Report to the North Carolina General Assembly, 1828." *Cotton History Review* 2 (January 1961): 52–67.

——. "An Origin of the New South: The South Carolina Homespun Company, 1808–1815." *Business History Review* 35 (Autumn 1961): 402–14.

——. "The Columbia Manufacturing Company and the Textile Industry of the District of Columbia, 1808–1816." *Maryland Historical Magazine* 57 (September 1962): 259–67.

——. "Reconstruction of the North Carolina Textile Industry, 1865–1885." *North Carolina Historical Review* 41 (January 1964): 34–53.

——. "Ante Bellum Industrial Foundations of the (Alleged) 'New South.' " *Textile History Review* 5 (August 1964): 22–43.

Griffin, Richard W., and Standard, Diffee W. "The Cotton Textile Industry in Ante-Bellum North Carolina. Part II. An Era of Boom and Consolidation, 1830–1860." *North Carolina Historical Review* 34 (April 1957): 131–64.

Hesseltine, William B. "Economic Factors in the Abandonment of Reconstruction." *Mississippi Valley Historical Review* 22 (September 1935): 191–210.

Kutler, Stanley I. "Chief Justice Taft, National Regulation and the Commerce Power." *Journal of American History* 51 (March 1965): 651–68.

Lander, Ernest M. "The Iron Industry in Ante-Bellum South Carolina." *Journal of Southern History* 20 (August 1954): 337–55.

Lanier, Joseph L. "The First Seventy-Five Years of West Point Manufacturing Company, 1880–1955." *Newcomen Society in North America* 14 (December 1955): 5–27.

Marmar, Theodore R. "Anti-Industrialism and the Old South: The Agrarian Perspective of John C. Calhoun." *Comparative Studies in Society and History* 9 (1966–1967): 377–406.

Martin, Thomas P. "Conflicting Cotton Interests at Home and Abroad, 1848–1857." *Journal of Southern History* 8 (May 1941): 173–94.

——. "The Advent of William Gregg and the Graniteville Company." *Journal of Southern History* 9 (August 1945): 389–423.

Moore, James T. "Redeemers Reconsidered: Change and Continuity in the Democratic South, 1870–1900." *Journal of Southern History* 44 (August 1978): 357–78.

Napier, John H. "Judge Edward McGehee, Cotton Planter, Pioneer Manufacturer and Mississippi Philanthropist." *Cotton History Review* 1 (January 1960): 27–28.

Patterson, Ernest F. "Cotton, the First Problem of United States Agriculture." *Cotton History Review* 1 (October 1960): 151–74.

Potter, David M. "The Historical Development of Eastern-Southern Freight Rate Relationships." *Law and Contemporary Problems* 14 (1947): 416–48.

Preyer, Norris W. "The Historian, the Slave, and the Ante-Bellum Textile Industry." *Journal of Negro History* 46 (April 1961): 67–82.

Ramsdell, Charles W. "The Control of Manufacturing by the Confederate Government." *Mississippi Valley Historical Review* 7 (December 1921): 221–49.

Rogers, William W. "The Farmers Alliance in Alabama." *Alabama Review* 15 (January 1962): 5–18.

Shugg, Roger W. "Survival of the Plantation System in Louisiana." *Journal of Southern History* 3 (August 1937): 311–25.

Steadman, Enoch. "A Brief Treatise on Manufacturing in the South, 1851." Rptd. in *Cotton History Review* 2 (April 1961): 103–18.

Turner, Frederick Jackson. "The Significance of the Section in American History." *Wisconsin Magazine of History* 8 (March 1925): 255–80.

Ward, Judson C. "The New Departure Democrats of Georgia: An Interpretation." *Georgia Historical Quarterly* 41 (September 1957): 227–36.

Webb, Elizabeth Y. "Cotton Manufacturing and State Regulations in North Carolina, 1861–1865." *North Carolina Historical Review* 9 (April 1932): 117–37.

Books

Albion, Robert G. *The Rise of the Port of New York, 1815–1860.* New York: Charles Scribner's Sons, 1939.

Allen, Robert L. *Reluctant Reformers: Racism and Social Reform Movements in the United States.* Washington, D.C.: Howard University Press, 1974.

Barbee, William J. *The Cotton Question.* New York: Metropolitan Record Office, 1866.

Beale, Howard K. *Theodore Roosevelt and the Rise of America to World Power.* New York: Macmillan Co., 1956.

Billings, Dwight B. *Planters and the Making of a "New South."* Chapel Hill: University of North Carolina Press, 1979.

Blicksilver, Jack. *Cotton Manufacturing in the Southeast: An Historical*

Analysis. Atlanta: Bureau of Business and Economic Research, Georgia State College of Business Administration, Bulletin No. 5, July 1959.

Buck, Paul H. *The Road to Reunion, 1865–1900.* Boston: Little, Brown and Co., 1937.

Campbell, Charles S. *Special Business Interests and the Open Door Policy.* New Haven: Yale University Press, 1951.

Cash, Wilbur J. *The Mind of the South.* New York: Alfred A. Knopf, 1941.

Clark, Victor S. *The History of Manufacturers in the United States*, vol. 2. New York: McGraw-Hill, 1929.

Commons, John R.; Phillips, Ulrich B.; Gilmore, Eugene A.; Summer, Helen L.; and Andrews, John B., eds. *A Documentary History of American Industrial Society.* Cleveland: Arthur H. Clark Co., 1909.

Cook, Harvey T. *The Life and Legacy of David Rogerson Williams.* New York: n.p., 1916.

Cooper, William J. *The Conservative Regime, South Carolina, 1877–1890.* Baltimore: Johns Hopkins University Press, 1968.

Copeland, Melvin T. *The Cotton Manufacturing Industry of the United States.* Cambridge: Harvard University Press, 1912.

Coulter, E. Merton. *The Confederate States of America, 1861–1865.* Baton Rouge: Louisiana State University Press, 1950.

Craven, Avery O. *Edmund Ruffin Southerner: A Study in Secession.* New York: A. Appleton and Co., 1932.

———. *The Coming of the Civil War.* Chicago: University of Chicago Press, 1957.

David, Paul, A.; Gutman, Herbert G.; Sutch, Richard; Temin, Peter; and Wright, Gavin. *Reckoning with Slavery.* New York: Oxford University Press, 1976.

DeCanio, Stephen J. *Agriculture in the Postbellum South.* Cambridge, Mass.: MIT Press, 1974.

Degler, Carl N. *The Other South.* New York: Harper & Row, 1974.

Eaton, Clement. *A History of the Southern Confederacy.* New York: Macmillan Co., 1954.

———. *The Growth of Southern Civilization, 1790–1860.* New York: Harper & Row, 1961.

Ferleger, Herbert R. *David A. Wells and the American Revenue System, 1865–1870.* New York: Columbia University Libraries, 1942.

Fogel, Robert; and Engerman, Stanley. *Time on the Cross.* New York: Little, Brown and Co., 1974.

Foner, Eric. *Free Soil, Free Labor, Free Men.* New York: Oxford University Press, 1970.

Foner, Philip S. *Business and Slavery: The New York Merchants and the Irrepressible Conflict.* Chapel Hill: University of North Carolina Press, 1941.

Frederickson, George M. *The Black Image in the White Mind.* New York: Harper & Row, 1971.

Freehling, William W. *Prelude to Civil War: The Nullification Controversy in South Carolina, 1816–1836.* New York: Harper & Row, 1965.

Gaston, Paul M. *The New South Creed: A Study in Southern Mythmaking.* Baton Rouge: Louisiana State University Press, 1970.

Gates, Paul W. *Agriculture and the Civil War.* New York: Alfred A. Knopf, 1965.

Genovese, Eugene D. *The Political Economy of Slavery.* New York: Pantheon Books, 1965.

———. *Roll, Jordan, Roll.* New York: Vintage Books, 1976.

———. *The World the Slaveowners Made.* New York: Vintage Books, 1976.

Gibb, George S. *The Saco-Lowell Shops: Textile Machine Building in New England, 1813–1959.* Cambridge: Harvard University Press, 1950.

Going, Allen J. *Bourbon Democracy in Alabama, 1874–1890.* Montgomery: University of Alabama Press, 1951.

Goodwyn, Lawrence. *Democratic Promise.* New York: Oxford University Press, 1976.

Hammond, M. B. *The Cotton Industry.* New York: Macmillan Co., 1897.

Hart, Roger L. *Redeemers, Bourbons, and Populists: Tennessee, 1870–1896.* Baton Rouge: Louisiana State University Press, 1975.

Hesseltine, William B. *Confederate Leaders in the New South.* Baton Rouge: Louisiana State University Press, 1950.

Houston, David F. *A Critical Study of Nullification in South Carolina.* Cambridge: Harvard University Press, 1896.

Jacobs, William P. *The Pioneer.* Clinton, S.C.: Jacobs and Co. Press, 1935.

Johnson, Gerald W. *The Making of a Southern Industrialist, A Biographical Study of Simpson Bobo Tanner.* Chapel Hill: University of North Carolina Press, 1952.

Jordan, Weymouth T. *Ante-Bellum Alabama, Town and Country.* Tallahassee: Florida State University, 1957.

———. *Rebels in the Making, Planters' Conventions and Southern Propaganda.* Tuscaloosa, Ala.: Confederate Publishing Co., 1958.

Kettell, Thomas P. *Southern Wealth and Northern Profits.* Tuscaloosa: University of Alabama Press, 1965.

Kibler, Lillian A. *Benjamin F. Perry, South Carolina Unionist.* Durham, N.C.: Duke University Press, 1946.

Knowlton, Evelyn H. *Pepperell's Progress, History of a Cotton Textile Company, 1844–1945.* Cambridge: Harvard University Press, 1948.

Kolchin, Peter. *First Freedom: The Response of Alabama's Blacks to Emancipation and Reconstruction.* Westport, Conn.: Greenwood Publishing Co., 1972.

La Feber, Walter. *The New Empire: An Interpretation of American Expansion.* Ithaca: Cornell University Press, 1963.

Lander, Ernest M. *The Textile Industry in Antebellum South Carolina.* Baton Rouge: Louisiana State University Press, 1969.

McCormick, Thomas J. *China Market, America's Quest for Informal Empire, 1893–1901.* Chicago: Quadrangle Books, 1967.

McLaurin, Melton A. *Paternalism and Protest: Southern Cotton Mill Workers and Organized Labor, 1875–1905.* Westport, Conn.: Greenwood Publishing Co., 1971.

McMath, Robert C. *Populist Vanguard.* Chapel Hill: University of North Carolina Press, 1975.

Mitchell, Broadus. *The Rise of Cotton Mills in the South.* Baltimore: Johns Hopkins University Press, 1921.

———. *William Gregg, Factory Master of the Old South.* Chapel Hill: University of North Carolina Press, 1928.

Navin, Thomas R. *The Whitin Machine Works since 1831.* Cambridge: Harvard University Press, 1950.

Noblin, Stuart. *Leonidas LaFayette Polk, Agrarian Crusader.* Chapel Hill: University of North Carolina Press, 1949.

North, Douglass C. *The Economic Growth of the United States, 1790–1860.* New York: W. W. Norton and Co., 1966.

Ramsdell, Charles W. *Behind the Lines in the Southern Confederacy.* Baton Rouge: Louisiana State University Press, 1944.

Ransom, Roger; and Sutch, Richard. *One Kind of Freedom: The Economic Consequences of Emancipation.* New York: Cambridge University Press, 1977.

Roark, James L. *Masters without Slaves: Southern Planters in the Civil War and Reconstruction.* New York: W. W. Norton and Co., 1977.

Rogers, George C. *Evolution of a Federalist, William Loughton Smith of Charleston, 1758–1812.* Columbia: University of South Carolina Press, 1962.

Rose, Willie Lee. *Rehearsal for Reconstruction: The Port Royal Story.* New York: Bobbs-Merrill Co., 1964.

Russell, Robert R. *Economic Aspects of Southern Sectionalism, 1840–1861.* Urbana: University of Illinois Press, 1924.

Sale, Kirkpatrick. *Power Shift.* New York: Vintage Books, 1975.

Saloutos, Theodore. *Farmer Movements in the South, 1865–1933.* Berkeley: University of California Press, 1960.

Schwab, John C. *The Confederate States of America 1861–1865: A Financial and Industrial History of the South during the Civil War.* New Haven: Yale University Press, 1901.

Schwartz, Michael. *Radical Protest and Social Structure.* New York: Academic Press, 1976.

Sharkey, Robert P. *Money, Class, and Party: An Economic Study of the Civil War and Reconstruction.* Baltimore: Johns Hopkins University Press, 1959.

Shugg, Roger W. *Origins of Class Struggle in Louisiana.* Baton Rouge: Louisiana State University Press, 1968.

Simpkins, Francis N. *South Carolina during Reconstruction.* Chapel Hill: University of North Carolina Press, 1932.

Skipper, Ottis C. *J. D. B. De Bow, Magazinist of the Old South.* Athens: University of Georgia Press, 1958.

Smith, Adam. *The Wealth of Nations.* New York: Random House, Modern Library, 1937.

Smith, Alfred G. *Economic Readjustment of an Old Cotton State, South Carolina, 1820–1860.* Columbia: University of South Carolina Press, 1958.

Stampp, Kenneth M. *And the War Came: The North and the Secession Crisis, 1860–61.* Chicago: University of Chicago Press, 1950.

———. *The Causes of the Civil War.* Englewood Cliffs, N.J.: Prentice-Hall, 1959.

Stanwood, Edward. *American Tariff Controversies in the Nineteenth Century,* vol. 1. New York: Houghton Mifflin, 1903.

Starobin, Robert S. *Industrial Slavery in the Old South.* New York: Oxford University Press, 1970.

Steadman, Enoch. *The Southern Manufacturer, Showing the Advantage of Manufacturing Cotton in the Fields Where It Is Grown.* Gallatin, Tenn.: Gray and Boyers, 1858.

Stover, John F. *The Railroads of the South, 1865–1900.* Chapel Hill: University of North Carolina Press, 1955.

Sydnor, Charles S. *The Development of Southern Sectionalism, 1819–1848.* Baton Rouge: Louisiana State University Press, 1967.

Taussig, Frank W. *Some Aspects of the Tariff Question.* Cambridge: Harvard University Press, 1915.

Thompson, Holland. *From the Cotton Field to the Cotton Mill: A Study of Industrial Transition in North Carolina.* New York: Macmillan Co., 1906.

Tindall, George B. *The Emergence of the New South, 1913–1945.* Baton Rouge: Louisiana State University Press, 1967.

Tompkins, Daniel A. *Cotton Mill, Commercial Features.* Charlotte, N.C.: published by the author, 1899.

———. *American Commerce, Its Expansion.* Charlotte, N.C.: published by the author, 1900.

Van Deusen, John G. *The Ante-Bellum Southern Commercial Conventions.* Durham, N.C.: Duke University Press, 1926.

———. *Economic Basis of Disunion in South Carolina.* New York: Columbia University Studies in History, 1928.

Ware, Caroline F. *Early New England Cotton Manufacture: A Study in Industrial Beginnings.* New York: Russell and Russell, 1966.

Wender, Herbert. *Southern Commercial Conventions, 1837–1859.* Baltimore: Johns Hopkins University Press, 1930.

Wiener, Jonathan M. *Social Origins of the New South: Alabama, 1860–1885.* Baton Rouge: Louisiana State University Press, 1978.

Williams, William A. *The Contours of American History.* Cleveland: World Publishing Co., 1961.

————. *The Tragedy of American Diplomacy.* New York: Dell Publishing Co., 1962.

————. *The Roots of the Modern American Empire.* New York: Random House, 1969.

Williamson, Gustavus G. *Textile Leaders of the South.* Columbia, S.C.: R.L. Bryan Co., 1963.

Williamson, Joel. *After Slavery: The Negro in South Carolina during Reconstruction.* Chapel Hill: University of North Carolina Press, 1965.

Woodman, Harold S. *King Cotton and His Retainers.* Lexington: University of Kentucky Press, 1967.

Woodward, C. Vann. *Origins of the New South, 1877–1913.* Baton Rouge: Louisiana State University Press, 1951.

————. *American Counterpoint.* New York: Little, Brown and Co., 1971.

Woolfolk, George R. *The Cotton Regency: The Northern Merchants and Reconstruction, 1865–1880.* New York: Bookmen Associates, 1958.

Wright, Gavin. *The Political Economy of the Cotton South.* New York: W. W. Norton Co., 1978.

Index